Praise for
You Rise Glorious

"In my life, both personally and professionally, Mike Fo[illegible] of inspiration and encouragement. You'll find bot[illegible]'ll also find humility, wisdom, and compassion. [illegible]ike and his work, you will be met with grace."

—JAMIE TWORKOWSKI, founder of To Wr[illegible]s and *New York Times* best-selling author of *If Y[illegible] Much*

"Mike's words are soaked in a special blend of grace, compassion, and clarity for living in God's love. Absolutely beautiful."

—MARK BATTERSON, *New York Times* best-selling author and pastor of National Community Church in Washington, DC

"Mike Foster has created a movement, and this is the official playbook. *You Rise Glorious* provides all of us an extra dose of hope and inspiration. Join the team, put on your jersey, get on the field, and be part of the second-chance community!"

—BRAD LOMENICK, former president of Catalyst and author of *The Catalyst Leader* and *H3 Leadership*

"Mike is your friend, whether you've ever met him or not. You can feel it on every page of this book, and Mike wrote it for you because he wants good for his friends. This book is a beautiful, healing thing, and I am so glad it exists."

—ANNIE F. DOWNS, best-selling author of *Looking for Lovely* and *Let's All Be Brave*

"What if we partied as much as we preached? This question from *You Rise Glorious* hit me like a ton of bricks, but it wasn't the only knee-buckling moment in the book. A lot of people write about grace, but Mike Foster celebrates it, creating a raucous call to a party everyone is invited to. If you've ever wondered if second chances are real and available, read this book."

—JON ACUFF, author of *Do Over* and *Stuff Christians Like*

"Mike Foster is a rare and necessary antenna for goodness and grace. Through this wonderful book that brims with vulnerability and wisdom, we can begin to wholly realize the concept of unconditional love. In *You Rise Glorious,* Foster so beautifully shares the greatest news anyone can hear: you are beloved."

—RYAN O'NEAL, Sleeping At Last

"Five stars! This is fierce and compassionate truth telling at its finest. *You Rise Glorious* is an incredible road map for fully experiencing the grace of God in a whole new way."

—JUD WILHITE, senior pastor of Central Christian Church in Las Vegas

"Each page of this book was designed to remind us of our incredible stories. It's the voice of a man I trust, whispering over our shoulders that our weirdness is wonderful and our quirks are among our most endearing qualities."

—BOB GOFF, Chief Balloon Inflator and *New York Times* best-selling author of *Love Does*

"Mike is this generation's Brennan Manning. His passion for helping us live as God's beloved is awe inspiring, and this manifesto for second-chance living is exactly what our world needs right now."

—GABE LYONS, author of *Good Faith* and founder of Q

"I loved this profound work of grace and the simple reminder that life can be cherished in the midst of our brokenness. *You Rise Glorious* will cause hearts to leap for joy as we imagine a world where our imperfect stories truly matter."

—REBEKAH LYONS, author of *Freefall to Fly*

"I don't read many books, but I always read Mike's. This one leads us back to the core of who we are and how we should live. Filled with vulnerability, hope, and practical help, *You Rise Glorious* is a must-read!"

—JEREMY COWART, founder of The Purpose Hotel, See University, and Help-Portrait

"The day I hit the lowest point in my life I made one phone call. It was to Mike. That phone call convinced me that I would rise again. And reading this book was like having that phone call all over again. This book is a manual for anybody who wants to rise again. I'm so grateful for Mike and this message."

—CARLOS WHITTAKER, a speaker and the author of *Moment Maker*

"*You Rise Glorious* is a profound and inspiring book that will stir your heart toward belief, bravery, and the life God dreams for you."

—SCOTT HARRISON, founder of charity: water

YOU RISE GLORIOUS

a wild invitation to live **fierce, free,** and **unstoppable** in a world that tries to break you, shame you, and tell you that you're not enough

ACCESS TO
FREE
"YOU RISE GLORIOUS"
E-COURSE
INSIDE

MIKE FOSTER

Foreword by Bob Goff

Previously released as *PEOPLE OF THE SECOND CHANCE*

WATERBROOK

You Rise Glorious

This book is not intended to replace the medical advice of a trained medical professional. Readers are advised to consult a physician or other qualified health-care professional regarding treatment of their medical problems. The author and publisher specifically disclaim liability, loss, or risk, personal or otherwise, which is incurred as a consequence, directly or indirectly, of the use or application of any of the contents of this book.

Details in some anecdotes and stories have been changed to protect the identities of the persons involved.

Trade Paperback ISBN 978-1-60142-855-4
Hardcover ISBN 978-1-60142-854-7
eBook ISBN 978-1-60142-856-1

Cover design by Kelly L. Howard and Brian Hurst

Published in the United States by WaterBrook, an imprint of the Crown Publishing Group, a division of Penguin Random House LLC, New York.

WaterBrook® and its deer colophon are registered trademarks of Penguin Random House LLC.

Originally published in hardcover and in slightly different form in the United States as *People of the Second Chance* by WaterBrook, an imprint of the Crown Publishing Group, a division of Penguin Random House LLC, in 2016.

The Cataloging-in-Publication Data is on file with the Library of Congress.

Printed in the United States of America
2018—First Trade Paperback Edition

10 9 8 7 6 5 4 3 2 1

Special Sales

Most WaterBrook books are available at special quantity discounts when purchased in bulk by corporations, organizations, and special-interest groups. Custom imprinting or excerpting can also be done to fit special needs. For information, please e-mail specialmarketscms@penguinrandomhouse.com or call 1-800-603-7051.

For every broken life becoming beautiful again

CONTENTS

FOREWORD

Mike and I have been teaching a class at a local university together. It's a class about success and failure and what we do with each. Truthfully, we spend a lot more time in class talking about failure than success. The reason is simple. Our successes often distract us, while our failures usually shape us.

Everyone wants to be successful. Whether you're a race car driver or business leader or Olympian, you long to repeat your successes. Who doesn't? But not many people want to repeat a failure.

Still, there are a handful of people who live their lives unafraid because they have come to realize the beauty in both success and failure. These people would rather fail trying than fail watching. Mike is one of those guys.

Each week in class we bring friends to talk about a time when they failed. In fact, experiencing failure has become almost a prerequisite to being our friend. Honestly, we wouldn't have much in common otherwise. We've noticed that people who have failed are more generous with their compassion, more extravagant with their love, and less inhibited in their expressions of both. I think it's because these people spend less time caring about what their lives look like and more time figuring out what their lives are about.

I love Disneyland. On my first trip there as a kid, my family stayed at the Disneyland Hotel. I'd saved up my allowance for a year, and on the first day I bought a stuffed animal with a really long, furry tail. That night we went out on the balcony to watch the fireworks. I gave my stuffed animal the best seat in the house—up on the railing. When the fireworks ended, I tried to pick up my nylon friend, but it wouldn't move. Someone below had grabbed ahold of my stuffed animal's tail. I pulled up as hard as I could, and he pulled down as hard as he could. I didn't know what to do. It was the first time I ever felt as if something precious was about to be taken from me.

This is a book about love and hope and tugging back against those things that are trying to steal our joy, our attention, and our identities. All of us will have something that has been relentless in its tug on our lives. It may be a bad religious experience, our political stance, or the failures or successes we've experienced. This book is about tugging back. It's an invitation, with a little muscle behind it, to see who God is turning us into, rather than overidentifying with who we were.

This isn't a self-help book about just being happy; it's about being aware of the beauty of becoming whole. It's not about finding meaning in our lives by looking perfect; instead, it's about realizing that we are perfectly loved and allowing this to give our lives meaning. This is a book for messed-up overcomers, for religious rebels, for the broken but resilient. It's not about taking a knee in the end zone when you win; it's about taking both when you don't.

Mike has created this grace-filled, shame-breaking book by riffing on the lessons he's been learning from Jesus and has been incorporating in a nonprofit organization he founded for people who have messed up. It's aptly named *People of the Second Chance*. It's made of people like you and like me who are pulling back against what's got us by the tail.

If you feel as if you've lost your way and have asked the questions I've asked myself so many times, such as "Who am I?" or "Why am I here?" or "What in my life will outlast me?" then this book will be a heart-gripping, life-changing page-turner for you. This book welcomes you into a community of second chancers who are discovering their true identity, their hopeful purpose, and the unfair advantage their failures have given them to impact others with big love rather than big opinions.

Here's the simple truth: life is messy. We don't need to act surprised anymore. Instead, we have reason to be tremendously hopeful. In the reverse economy of Jesus, the things that break us, God inverts to shape us. Either we can let those things pull us over the rail, or we can start pulling back. Fear, shame, and worthlessness have only the power we give them. This book is about hope, love, and grace and how through them all we can rise glorious.

Each page of this book was designed to remind us of our incredible stories. It's the voice of a man I trust, whispering over our shoulders that our weirdness is wonderful and our quirks are among our most endearing qualities. Most important, this book reminds us that God is just moments away from transforming the shame and fear we've allowed to pull us over the rails into a right perspective about self-acceptance, love, and faith.

I'm proud to introduce you to my friend Mike Foster and the safe place he's made in this book for all of us to learn, grow, and explore our successes and our failures. You're already accepted and loved, and you've only just arrived. That's because there's nothing to prove, nothing to be except you, and everything to imagine. This is a place where the dream God has placed in your heart isn't limited by the failures you've encountered in getting here.

Welcome home.

—Bob Goff, Chief Balloon Inflator and *New York Times* best-selling author of *Love Does*

THE DISEASE OF *loneliness* INFECTS US ALL. IT'S A *dark* DEADLY PLAGUE. *friendship* IS THE CURE.

MIKE FOSTER

Introduction

Three Seconds

I am a second chancer. And it only took three seconds of my life to make me long for that role.

It was a Memorial Day weekend on the Colorado River, and I was nineteen years old. I joined some families from church who were doing their annual water-ski trip. The Rogers and MacGregor families put on a water-skiing extravaganza each year and invited a few friends. I got to be a chosen friend that year.

We woke early the first morning and water-skied for a few hours. Everyone fared well except for me, a newbie. When I skied, I looked more like a drunk giraffe than a musclebound water aficionado. I gave it my best shot, but I'm certain I swallowed more water than I skied on.

Everyone on the boat played cool about my tragic shortcomings in the ski department. No flat-out mocking. Just some heavy sighing and huffing with a dash of disdain.

My pride was bruised, but I kept up a good image. I've always been good at image managing and pretending to be okay. I learned early on that it's best to be strong and smile your way through subpar performances. Nothing to see here, folks. I'm fine. No weakness at all. None. Let's just move along.

Furthermore, I couldn't let any of those girls in Christian bikinis know I wasn't potential boyfriend material. Know what I mean?

Ryan MacGregor, my friend who invited me on the trip, sensed my ego had been bumped around a little. He figured it would be good for me to give boat driving a shot. I could redeem my honor and build up what was left of my bruised ego. I needed a second chance. So Ryan asked, "Hey, Mike, you want to drive the boat?"

I honestly thought, *How hard could this boat-driving thing be? It's got a steering wheel. I know how to do steering wheels.*

I said, "Sure, Ryan. Count me in."

He explained that he would get the boat going. There is an art to pulling a skier out of the water, and as the rookie driver, I wasn't quite ready for that.

We started cruising up the river. John, our skier, zipped back and forth behind the boat. He skied like a graceful water gazelle, lightly jumping from one wave to another, so unlike the intoxicated-giraffe style I had demonstrated earlier that morning.

The warm wind blew in our faces. I felt alive.

Ryan gave me the look and said, "Okey-dokey, Mike. Your turn!" He scooted away from the wheel and pointed for me to take over. I did. Now I was driving, studly as can be. I was good with steering wheels. I hoped those Christian girls were noticing.

After a few moments our skier motioned that he wanted to turn around and go the other way. Ryan said, "Okay, Mike, we need to turn the boat and go back down the river. Just turn the wheel slowly and evenly, and you should be good to go."

So I began to turn the wheel and drive the boat into what I thought was clear water.

But it wasn't clear water.

There was a skier from another boat in my path. He had dropped into the water, waiting for his boat to pick him up. I didn't see him until it was too late. I couldn't turn our boat in time.

And I hit him.

It happened in just three seconds, yet it felt like an eternity. Ryan quickly cut the engines and dove into the water and swam toward the skier I had just hit. The skier's head flopped forward. His body bobbed on the water like a rag doll. A pool of red blood surrounded him. His life was draining into the water.

Panic. Fear. The Christian girls were now screaming.

And I just wanted to run.

Run as far and fast as I could from what I had done. Run from myself. Run from life. Run from what everyone was now thinking. Run from the fact that there was no going back. No undoing this. No repairing the damage. Just me facing a motionless, bloody body in the river. I wanted to escape.

Maybe you've been there too.

The skier survived. The doctors weren't sure how he survived, but he did. He lost a ton of blood. The propeller had snapped off and hit him in the head. The blade carved up his right arm. It was a miracle he was alive. The doctors said that if the propeller had struck just a quarter of an inch deeper, the force would have decapitated him.

That thought still gives me shivers.

My victim spent weeks in the hospital.

After the accident I was lost. I didn't know what to say. I didn't know how to act. How sad or strong are you supposed to be? There is no playbook for such tragedies.

Should I be grateful that he lived or regret the incredible damage I did? Do I talk about it or just keep quiet? Is there a Bible verse to hang on to? What should I feel? These are questions I later learned that only grace could answer.

Meanwhile, my heart was dead. I felt alone, and my thoughts were dark. My words stuck inside me, trapped in a story I desperately wanted to escape.

The damage I did that day on the river was real. It rippled through families, friends, and innocent bystanders. I would never forget, but they couldn't either.

Even though it was an unintentional accident, I still blamed myself. I took all the responsibility for that day. I shamed myself *hard* in the weeks and months that followed. The district attorney pressed criminal charges. A lawsuit followed. But none of that compared to my self-imposed punishment.

And out of this tragedy, I created a new rule for my life. Even though I loved being in, on, and around the water, it was now off-limits to me. I carved this final verdict on my heart so I would never, ever forget. The water was now closed to me. I told myself this would honor my victim. I also convinced myself this was the best way to protect my heart from having those feelings again. The new rule would work so well. It all made perfect sense.

Until it didn't.

Because that rule, meant to crush my shame and protect my heart, instead crushed me. I wrote it to protect myself, but I ended up punishing myself, pinning myself down to a small, groveling life. I couldn't take the chance of stirring any more troubles on the waters of my story. I became small and I played it safe.

Such rules and laws. It was like making a deal with the devil. No more sorrow at the cost of no joy.

And that's the problem, isn't it? Grace gets censored when we write these devilish decrees for our lives. Secret commandments get scrawled on personal tablets of shame, and we live life as if our stories belong on a discount rack rather than as valued, cherished children of God. We let a moment of pain cut us off from a lifetime of grace.

The rules we write for ourselves are sneaky. They run quietly in the background like a virus infecting an operating system. We forget they are even there. They intertwine their devious codes throughout our spiritual, emotional, and psychological systems. I call them the Five Condemnments:

1. I don't deserve a second chance.
2. I am my shame. I am my secrets.
3. I will always feel and be this way.
4. I am defined by my worst moments.
5. My life, my dreams, my hopes no longer matter.

And this is what we need to talk about, isn't it? We need to look at what's running in the background of our beliefs and expose the shame virus corrupting our hope for a better life. We must come out of the shadows and talk about hard things.

REACHING BACK

When I am working with hurting people, probably the most tragic thing I witness is when they have accepted the lie that whatever ugly, can't-talk-about-it, embarrassing thing has happened in their stories is somehow beyond the grace of God. That his mercy doesn't reach far enough. That his hand of grace is just beyond . . .

- the quiet addiction to painkillers;
- the shame of an unexpected divorce from the person you loved so much;
- someone's sexuality and what it all means;
- the betrayal of a family member;
- the fear of growing old and being alone.

God's reach is just beyond . . .

- a secret abortion and the sorrows of miscarriages;
- the depression, the sadness, and the eating disorder;

- the drinking and the bad choices;
- hidden regrets that you chose your career instead of your kids.

Yet God is reaching out in all these painful moments and whispers, *Just reach back to me, my beloved! I am here. Please, I beg you. Just reach back.*

In preparing to write this book, I thought about you a lot. About what your life might look like right now. Where do you live? What hurts do you carry? Do you like yourself? What beliefs do you have? Whom do you love? Who loves you? What lies do you believe? What friends do you have? Do you know the lavish grace of God?

I wondered why you might pick up a book about second chances. Were you looking for . . .

- a chance to change?
- a chance to thrive?
- a chance to be challenged?
- a chance to start over?
- a chance to forgive?
- a chance to dream wild dreams?

Or maybe you're looking for a chance to be loved as you've never been loved before. And wouldn't that be wonderful? Because to be loved like that is what you were made for. It's the reason you and I are here. It's what we are all looking for. And that, my friend, is the place we must start.

There are two big ideas I will talk about in the pages ahead. They are the foundation for what I believe it means to rise glorious. They are the values on which I try to base my own life. And I have found that if we embrace them, they will take us into the house of grace and belonging.

Fundamentally, this book rests on answering these questions that every human being has asked thousands of times:

Who am I?
What am I here for?

There are many answers to these two questions. Countless gurus, parents, religious leaders, motivational speakers, infomercial pitchmen, and those who are trying to sell something for three easy payments of $19.99 seem to have an answer for you. But let me be bold for a moment. Let me take a stab at answering these most basic human questions the best way I know how. Let me answer through the lens of God's love and what I know of my own brokenness.

THE HUMBLE ARROGANCE OF BEING HIS BELOVED

My simplistic answer to the question "Who am I?" is this: my truest, purest, nonnegotiable identity is the beloved. And in spite of my checkered past, my fabulous flops, my painful history, my deepest flaws, my bonehead screwups, and, yes, even beyond my own beliefs about myself, I am God's beloved. This is my foundational identity and the foundational identity of every human being.

I am not those three seconds on the Colorado River. You are not your failures. And just because we have *made* mistakes doesn't mean we *are* mistakes. Every other self-concept is a jumbled concoction of our fears, insecurities, and hurtful words spoken over our lives.

"Define yourself radically as one beloved by God," said Brennan Manning. "This is the true self. Every other identity is illusion."[1]

Identity is the engine that drives the relationship not only with ourselves but also with God and others. If your identity is broken, your life is broken. If you define it incorrectly, you will carry that wrong definition into your story. If all you see are your limitations, you will miss out on the stunning possibilities God is creating in front of you.

I have heard it said that the only thing needed for a powerful lion to be intimidated by a person with a whip is for the lion to forget who he is. If the lion forgets he is a lion, he is doomed to a life of controlled captivity.

Your beliefs about who you are have more power than you likely realize. Think about this: you can never—and I mean *never*—live above your self-imposed limitations. If you think you can't do something, you can't and never will. Period. You won't rise above your own negative self-image.

Let me share an example.

On the first day of school, in an after-school program, the predominantly African American children in Oakland, California, hear something none of them has ever heard before. They learn that the word *Africa* wasn't always spelled A-f-r-i-c-a but earlier was spelled A-f-r-a-c-a. The children are asked to speculate why it might have been changed and whether it matters. They shrug their shoulders as if to say, "Who knows?" After all, what difference can one letter make?

The teacher then explains that the syllable *fric* can be traced back to an Arab word meaning "land of the conquered or vanquished" but the syllable *frac* goes back to a term that means "land of the hidden soul."

The teacher asks again: "Do you think it matters?" For someone with Afracan heritage, one letter is the difference between seeing oneself as a vanquished victim or a descendant of humanity's "hidden soul."

That's how these kids in Oakland begin a year of life-changing lessons, not just in history and colonialism, but also in empowerment and identity. It's too soon to draw conclusions, but so far all the children who have gone through this yearlong after-school program are showing high levels of engagement in their learning and significant academic improvement.[2]

What if you changed a letter in your identity? Could a few tweaks in who you think you are be the beginning of a whole new story? Could identity hold the key to letting hope and healing rush in? Could stepping away from stinking thinking radically change the way you see yourself and your role in the world? I think it will.

It's time to stop seeing yourself as an inhabitant in the land of the conquered and vanquished. That's not you. You are from the land of the hidden soul.

You are not made to live under the weight of religion or guilt or chronic not-enough-ness. You are made to enjoy the love of God.

His heart is far larger, his love far stronger than anything we can imagine. A relationship with him is not a relationship between equals. He runs the show. He initiates; he works; he finishes. That's scary. God is one lover you cannot manipulate or woo. He's all one sided. It's all grace. And he is all love.

PARTY PLANNERS

So if the starting point of second-chance living is knowing *who we are,* then the next step is knowing *what we are to be about.* Franciscan priest Richard Rohr says, "When you get your 'Who am I?' question right, all the 'What should I do?' questions tend to take care of themselves."[3]

It is so easy to complain about the state of the world. Violence. Selfishness. Economic injustice. Racism. Sexism. Systemic oppression.

The reality is, bombs, bureaucracies, and political parties will not solve society's greatest problems. Only you and I can solve them, and we can do it with subversive acts of love. That means you and I must believe again in the world, in ourselves, and in each other.

I love what author Howard Zinn wrote in his essay "The Optimism of Uncertainty."

> If we see only the worst, it destroys our capacity to do something. If we remember those times and places—and there are so many—where people have behaved magnificently, this gives us the energy to act, and at least the possibility of sending this spinning top of a world in a different direction. And if we do act, in however small a way, we don't have to wait for some grand utopian future. The future is an infinite succession of presents, and to live now as we think human beings should live, in defiance of all that is bad around us, is itself a marvelous victory.[4]

So how do we respond to being the beloved? What will our hours, days, and lifetimes be filled with as we sink deeper and deeper into the knowledge of his love? Or as the poet Mary Oliver asked,

> Tell me, what is it you plan to do
> with your one wild and precious life?[5]

The response to God's love is before us. I think it is clear, but we often miss it.

I see God as someone who loves to play, dream, and create. He is the one who hung sparkling stars in the night sky and paints masterpiece sunsets each evening. I see God as a friend who smiles and laughs and likes cupcakes with chocolate icing. He is the life *and* the God of the party.

I love how the Scriptures point out that Jesus himself was so prone to have a good time that he was accused of being "a glutton and a drunkard" (Matthew 11:19). Or consider the clearest picture of God's grace, in the parable of the prodigal son. The whole point of the gospel comes through a story about a wayward child who returns home to a raging party thrown in his honor. Given by whom? The father, who clearly represents God. The Creator celebrates broken things as a way to love us. And this, my friend, is also what he invites us to do.

Yet too often we've missed this part, haven't we? Sometimes we see the sin but forget about the celebration. We lick our wounds but never a tasty sprinkled cupcake. Instead of prodigal parties with reggae music and fruit punch, we throw pity parties that no one wants to attend. We've grown so victimized by our own hurting that we've missed celebrating the miracle of our healing. And not only our own healing but also the healing of those around us.

Second chancers must find the party. We must be the party. We must create opportunities to celebrate and become the proverbial hostess with the mostest.

What I am proposing is that you and I do the work of prodigal party planning. That we figure out creative ways to celebrate the uncelebrated people in our cities. That we look at our fellow prodigals and say, "Yeah, we've been there too. It hurts. It stinks. But you're loved, and here's a cupcake."

The formula could look like this: *people* of the second chance become *planners* of the second chance. The beloved who adopt the sole purpose and mission to love. Get your address book out.

Open up your Google contacts. Look around you. Send out invitations to . . .

- misfits and outsiders;
- single moms and welfare dads;
- enemies and friends, haters and lovers;
- ex-cons and crack dealers;
- Wal-Mart greeters and Rolex-wearing CEOs;
- dreamers, doubters, and everyone in between.

Let's just say that everyone gets an invite and no one gets left out.

Mother Teresa said, "The problem with the world is that we draw the circle of our family too small."[6] When we plan parties, we should draw big circles, because we are all family, and everyone needs a party.

Imagine what our faith might look like if we partied as much as we preached. If we spent as much time blowing up balloons as we do attending Bible studies. What might happen if our mission were to serve as much cheese dip to crazies as we do communion to churchgoers?

It is time to enjoy God again. Yes, there is suffering, but there is also celebration. Yes, there is pain, but there is also a party. Your life will be heavy, and it will be light. The question is, How will you carry it, and what will you do with it? A friend told me that the exact same place can be either a prison or a promised land. The difference is perspective and the fact that you must work to make where you are where you want to be.

Looking back on my boating accident, I know I could have used a prodigal party. I needed something to free me from the prison where my heart was being held. Someone sharing some chips and salsa with me would have been my miracle. I needed God's beloved to let me know the Father still delighted in me. I eventually forgave myself and, in recognition of this, let myself enjoy the water again, but it took many years.

People need to know that after the tragic pain, the irreplaceable loss, the death of our dreams, reputations, innocence, and health; after battling the storms of addiction, betrayal, and boat accidents; after we've messed up, fallen flat on our faces, and tasted the bitter pill of our own powerlessness—after all of this, we can smile again.

The American diplomat John Kenneth Galbraith said, "All successful revolutions are the kicking in of a rotten door."[7] I want this book to be a big boot and the systems of shame, cynicism, hopelessness, judgment, captivity, and oppression to be the rotten door.

The tragedy of my boating accident and my other rock-bottom experiences have taught me many lessons about what it means to live as a second chancer who refuses to settle for anything less than a life that rises glorious. This is the journey I want to take you on.

I've seen the power of believing in broken people. I've discovered that the only thing I have to be is God's beloved. I am not those three seconds, and with the God of grace by my side, I'm ready to kick down the rotten door.

When we speak our true stories, we are left with something real: you and me. My story and yours. The truth that sets us free.

Mike Foster

One

Green Coats

Whether we like it or not, our experience is one part mischief, one part miracle, and one part mayhem all slammed together to make this cocktail called life. Our second-chance stories can look very different from one another and yet are often similar. Life demands that you and I sit in the tension of pain and suffering.

One of the first steps of living as a second chancer is to get comfortable with our messes. To find a peace with who we are and what life turned into for us. I've sat with so many people who have struggled with the sorrow of their stories, whose expectations did not line up with how life had turned out. They wanted an outcome that was never promised.

My simple advice to them? Embrace it all. Every tear and every heartbreak. Every stain and every scab. Every flaw and every imperfection. They belong to you, I say, so wear them with your head held high.

Second chancers understand our brokenness isn't something to hide but to integrate into our lives. We do not need to be ashamed. No matter what the world says, we are not "less than" for being broken.

And yet it is so tempting to have it all together, isn't it? To look so good and be so fine. The right clothes. The right brands. Sexy Instagram photos where we look thin and young. Our perfect kids winning student-of-the-month awards. Pictures of our summer vacations that are better than everyone else's summer vacations. Fat girls want to be skinny girls, and skinny guys want to be beefier guys. We nip and tuck and Photoshop almost every aspect of our lives. It is the perfection playbook.

God's desire is to unleash you and me from the pathological desire to look nice. He says, "Whoever you are, whatever you look like, whatever mess you've been in, don't worry about that anymore. You're mine, and you're in good hands now."

He meets us when our faces are smudged with last night's sin. In the stink of old cigarettes, cheap booze, and the Pine-Sol we used to clean our vomit off the floor. He is there in our shame and self-hatred. He meets us in the middle of our secrets—those things we lie about when we say they are no big deal.

My fellow second chancers, I know we all want to look good, but we're not meant to look that good. The grace movement is built on imperfection and scraggly edges.

Without stains and scars, hope is an afterthought. A luxury instead of a necessity. Without our imperfections, there is nothing to place in the hands of God.

WE ARE ALL GREEN COATS

In 1955 a woman named Elizabeth Henson was cleaning out her wardrobe closet. She felt it was time to discard some items that were old or that she didn't wear anymore. Pieces in which the colors had faded, the edges had come undone, and over the years they had grown to smell of mothballs and mildew.

As Elizabeth was working through her closet, she came across a green coat she no longer wanted. Its time had come and gone. The fuzzy and frayed lightweight jacket was now a throwaway.

To her surprise, someone wanted the old coat. Her college-age son asked if he could have it.

I'm sure she must have thought, *Why in the world would you want this old, worthless thing?* But even though his request didn't make sense, she was more than willing to hand over the fuzzy green garment.

And as the story goes, with great delight her son brought the throwaway coat into his workshop. He grabbed a needle and thread and a pair of scissors. He carefully shaped the jacket into his vision. He sewed and stitched. He also grabbed a Ping-Pong ball and cut it into halves for eyes.

I'm sure back in 1955 no one could have imagined that Elizabeth's discarded green coat would go on to become an international pop icon, date a prima-donna pig, and play an Oscar-nominated song on a banjo in a swamp. But you see, Elizabeth Henson's son was named Jim. And that old green coat she was ready to throw away became the very first Kermit the Frog.

This is what happens when we put our throwaways into the hands of God. He has a vision for our brokenness. He crafts something surprising out of it.

We may not see how our frayed, smelly imperfections can be redesigned, but God certainly can. He believes that our imperfections are the raw materials for crafting something extraordinary. Second chances create banjo-playing frogs out of old green coats. They take imperfect people and give them a purpose.

Jim believed the coat could become Kermit. God believes your flaws can become a beautiful new you.

THE BEAUTIFUL LIE

And yet we believe what I call the *beautiful lie.*

The lie says this is what really counts: to be wealthy, powerful, influential, attractive, admired, talented, popular, and, above all, valuable. We must make a life that is worth something to others. Worth more than others. The world screams at us to hurry up and matter. Our lives become a reaction to this lie.

We must not be nothings. To be good for nothing is to be as good as dead. And death is what we fear most. The death that says our lives have no value.

So we thrash about in a pool of comparison and one-upmanship. Our lives become burdened by the heaviness of getting it right. Our joy becomes brittle, and our hearts slowly break. The only possible outcome of this hurry-up-and-matter hustle is the slow crushing of our souls.

But God offers real life, where our brokenness is redeemed. He says we can abandon society's beautiful lie and allow him to breathe new life into us, his beloved.

I think of the passage in Ezekiel where the Lord leads the prophet through a valley. Ezekiel wrote: "GOD's Spirit took me up and set me down in the middle of an open plain strewn with bones. He led me around and among them—a lot of bones! There were bones all over the plain—dry bones, bleached by the sun" (37:1–2, MSG).

And God tells Ezekiel to prophesy, to reveal something by divine inspiration, over these bleached and broken things. He does a Jim Henson power move, and the bones come alive.

Bones come alive. Green coats come alive. Broken things

made beautiful. God breathes life into our dead and imperfect things.

LIFE IS MORE THAN LIVING AND THEN DYING

If you're dissatisfied with your life, perhaps it's because you haven't discovered the delight of flaunting your flaws. If you feel exhausted, perhaps it's because you've been fighting so hard to get it right and measure up. If you're bored with your story, maybe it's because perfection is perfectly boring. Or as writer Anne Lamott quipped, "Perfect means shallow and unreal and fatally uninteresting." She also wrote that "perfectionism is the voice of the oppressor."[1] Looking good is no fun at all.

I recently read about a community in communist-controlled North Korea.[2] The town of Kijong-dong is just across the demilitarized zone from the neighboring South Korea. The community is filled with beautiful white buildings with light-blue roofs.

From a distance Kijong-dong looks like a prosperous community. And that's what the communist regime of North Korea wants you to believe. The town has been specifically designed to resemble a thriving village, supposedly to lure possible defectors from the south.

But on closer inspection you would notice that the buildings have no glass in the windows. Automatic timers turn the lights on and off. No one actually lives in Kijong-dong. It is only a facade of a flourishing town. It is a lie.

Too often our stories are facades made to look as if we are flourishing. Let's consider the Sunday morning church ritual.

Wake up.

Shower and brush your teeth.

Comb your hair better than you did Saturday.

Put on a matching outfit instead of just clothes.

Show up on time. Don't leave before the sermon is over.

Smile and be nice.

Prepare to repeat the process on Wednesday evening.

The world would be a different place if people were always as nice as they are at church on Sundays.

I used to work at a church where excellence was one of the organization's top values. I never really liked that value. It doesn't seem to fit in the kingdom of God. When our churches look, feel, and operate more like an Apple Store than a soup kitchen, we might be missing the point. God's kingdom is more trailer park than country club.

Second chancers must categorically reject this got-it-together spirituality. We must avoid buying into the American Dream and living this type of story.

For example, you start off as a kid, and life is fun. Bugs, butterflies, and Saturday-morning cartoons are all that matter. No cares in the world. Nothing to prove. Then you grow into a moody teenager, and school is either loads of fun or sheer torture—seemingly the only two choices of adolescence. You figure out that high school is just a painful social experiment with you as a guinea pig. Educationally, it's sort of a waste of time. Anybody still know how to do algebra? I don't.

Next, you go to college or join the work force and get serious about a guy or girl. You might marry, or you might wait, depending on your student loan debt and what your career prospects look like. Eventually you get a decent job. Buy a house. Fill it with a couch and the biggest flat-screen television you can afford. Have some kids. Then the kids leave. Then you're alone, and you wonder what happened to the past twenty-five years of your life. Your spouse feels like a stranger or a distant friend, not a lover or someone you're even that interested in now.

When you're successful in life, you buy shiny grown-up toys

and go on exotic vacations and maybe upgrade from your first spouse to a more advanced model. If you don't upgrade your spouse, you definitely upgrade your car. Then your body starts to break down, your hair thins and grays, and your bones creak. You Botox the wrinkles or suck fat out of fatty places. You go to Cross-Fit three times a week. Or maybe you just give up and enjoy yourself by saddling up to the local buffet on Tuesdays and Thursdays and numb your sorrows by eating more ice cream than you should. And then it's just a waiting game for death. And then it's over.

They call it the American Dream. I call it a generic waste of a life. It is our own version of Kijong-dong buildings. It is an empty story that, quite frankly, is not compelling. It is safe, heart numbing, and the product of perfectionism, performance, and striving for success.

The only way to prevent our lives from falling into this drudgery is to surrender our green coats to God. We must allow him to craft something wild, mysterious, and mind blowing with both our successes and failures.

THE FUTILITY OF TOOTHPASTE

You may be reading this and thinking, *Sure, Mike. That sounds nice. But I've got stuff in my life that isn't just some small flaw but a complete disaster.*

Perhaps the beginning of your second chance is not a flaunting of your flaws but a basic form of acceptance. For you, it means coming to peace with what is and with what may never change. I call them *life's irreversible moments,* the moments that you can't fix and that God wants to heal over a lifetime. There is no undoing or getting over them, only a journey to acceptance. They are life's toothpaste moments because, no matter how hard we try, the toothpaste ain't going back into the tube.

I know. I've tried. Not gonna happen. Ever. Once it's out, it's out.

So what's the toothpaste you've been trying to clean up? What have you been trying to get back into a tube only to be frustrated by the futility of even thinking you could? It looks different for all of us.

You chose an abuser instead of a lover.

Friends betrayed you and humiliated you for laughs.

Your childhood disintegrated into chaos as Mom and Dad despised each other.

Cancer attacked your body, and chemo joined in for fun.

Addiction stripped you of your dignity and your smile.

Your child took his life.

Whatever the event was, the toothpaste squirted out, and now there's a mess.

As I shared in the introduction, one of my greatest empty-tube experiences was the boating accident. There is no undoing the tragedy. No unfeeling the heartbreak. No recovering what was lost or taken. No place to hide from that mess. There is no taking back the damage I caused.

When we have these kinds of stories, it's scary. It's often humiliating. But we don't have to fear anything when we realize that all things, even the painful moments, are teaching us something. It is in the mess that God meets us.

The most healing thing we can do right now is admit we need help. We can't fix it. Our mirage of perfection and self-sufficiency has collapsed.

I learned this the hard way. The long way.

That three-second accident stole years of my life.

Had I made amends? Yes.

Had I owned the responsibility for that day? Yes.

Had I faced my mistake head-on? Yes.

But it was still a mess. It was because of this moment I learned the magic of a second chance.

When the toothpaste won't go back in the tube, brush your teeth.

WHY BRUSHING YOUR TEETH CHANGES EVERYTHING

When I share my boating story, sometimes people want to know if I was ever able to talk to the person I hit. Did we have some moment when I said "I'm sorry" and he said "I forgive you" and then we hugged and cried? It's how we imagine the story should go. But it didn't go that way at all. I never saw him again. Lawyers got involved, and due to litigation we never met. The victim has always been a shadow in my story. I can only see his wet face and the look in his eyes after the accident. I can only see his limp body being pulled into the boat. That moment is our only connection.

And though I wish the beginning and middle and end were more Hollywoodish or Christianish, the story lands like a thud for some people. It is what it is. A tragedy. A dark moment.

Do you have things in your story right now that feel unresolved? Are the details and the reasons and those elusive answers still fuzzy? Maybe you've battled all your life to find meaning for what happened in your past. And what happens if it never comes? Seriously, my beloved, it may never, ever come. Ultimately, we have to learn to be okay with that possibility.

THE LAND OF CARDBOARD AND SPOILS

Years ago I had a speaking engagement with Dieter Zander, a dynamic speaker and musician. He served at one of the most influential churches in America. Thousands of young adults came weekly to hear him teach. I was in awe of the God he spoke of and his ideas for the kingdom. He was truly gifted and on fire with God's blessing.

One night Dieter went to bed and woke up unable to speak or to move one of his arms. He had suffered a stroke from a condition called aphasia. The stroke wiped out his language hard drive and caused severe paralysis in his left arm. Unable to communicate and now living with a physical disability, Dieter was left with no choice but to resign from his preaching ministry.

He was forced to find new work. He took a job at Trader Joe's. His new duties were to mop the floors and take the expired food to the Salvation Army.

The world looked at Dieter and wrote him off. He was an old green coat. What good was a musician who couldn't play? A preacher who couldn't preach? But what did God say to Dieter? What does Dieter say about God?

After years of intense therapy, he began to regain some words. He says, "God was my boss. God is my friend now. God says, 'Dieter, you are not going to work. Now we play.'"

Recently LaDonna Witmer wrote a poem about Dieter and his story called "A Kingdom of Cardboard and Spoils."

> If I am the king of all I survey, then I am king
> of cardboard and spoils.
> My kingdom is a noisy, windowless room in the
> back of a Trader Joe's grocery store. . . .
>
> . . . .
>
> My kingdom used to be a stage. A microphone.
> A piano and an audience of thousands. . . .
> Then came the stroke.
> Now, five days a week, I arrive at Trader Joe's in the
> early dark, hours before the sun cracks the horizon.

I push my mop up and down aisles. . . . There is
no audience in this kingdom.
But that's ok, because I'm not performing. . . .
I'm just me. Just Dieter. . . .
There's something beautiful about this simple,
menial work, though.
Take the food marked as "spoils," for example. It's
all still good. The fruit is good, the meat is good,
the flowers are good. But they're not perfect. . . .
So the Trader Joe's employees fill shiny carts
with all this perfectly edible imperfection and
wheel the load back to my kingdom. From
there, it will go to feed the hungry, who won't
care at all that their apple is lopsided. . . . They
just want to eat.

. . . .

I understand the spoils. I can relate. Because I,
too, am spoiled. Over, and over and over again.
I used to be packaged as perfect. . . .
But now . . . I relish the imperfection. . . .

. . . .

But the cardboard is recycled. The spoils are
feeding the hungry.
And today I am thinking life is good.
It's very good.[3]

Dieter's story teaches us so much. It invites us to live for an audience of one. It teaches us that life is never packaged up nicely. And if we can be honest, most of us look like lopsided apples.

I could take a thousand showers, but the stain of my boating accident is not coming off. The stain can only be reimagined through the handiwork of God.

Friend, fellow imperfectionist, and second chancer, there is no need to clean up or get your act together. Just let God bring you into his workshop and rework your old green coat. Bring what you have, no matter what it looks like. His standards are embarrassingly low, and he will work with everything you're willing to put into his hands. You are imperfect, but you can be perfectly loved and perfectly used by him.

WHEN God writes
our STORIES, there
are NEVER mistakes,
just movements
to BRING us closer
to Him

MIKE FOSTER

Two

Return Home

It is the absurdity of God on full display. It goes like this. The morning sunrise needs the black night to truly shine. Violent Fridays lead to Easter Sundays. Resurrection can only follow death. Joy is sweetest after sorrow. I may not like the formula, but God sure doesn't seem to mind.

I wished I had learned this basic truth earlier in my own journey: *the pathway to the second-chance life is to wreck the first one.* It all must break to be made whole again.

We're the only creatures in God's creation who miss this universal truth. Growth universally comes through change, and change comes through pain. It is God's process. Does a caterpillar question the steps to becoming a butterfly? Does the seed challenge the plan for becoming a rose? Death, my fellow second chancer, is the nonnegotiable for flourishing and stepping into a life of love, hope, and faith. There is no other way.

Author Cynthia Occelli wrote: "For a seed to achieve its greatest expression, it must come completely undone. The shell cracks, its insides come out and everything changes. To someone who doesn't understand growth, it would look like complete destruction."[1]

Our hearts crack open.

Our souls crack open.

Our minds crack open.

It is through the cracks that God's love and light come in. And the light illuminates the truest you or me. It allows us to see who we really are. The beloved.

The second-chance life is about getting busy dying so we can get busy living. And as Jesus so plainly stated, "If you let your life go, you will save it" (Luke 17:33).

What I've learned in my own grace story is that losing everything is the entry fee for the prodigal party that God invites us to. Tickets can be picked up only in the valley of death. You can't find them anywhere else. Trust me, I've looked. StubHub. eBay. Willy Wonka chocolate bars. Amazon. Church. The tickets aren't there. We find them only in the blackest, deepest brokenness of our pain and loss.

WHEN DEATH KNOCKS ON THE DOOR

As a nineteen-year-old I went to the river to enjoy myself that day. To impress girls in bikinis. To show my tribe that I was fun, worthy, desirable. But after those three seconds on that day, a darkness fell over me—the same kind of darkness that falls over every life and must fall for true light to dawn. Death knocked on my door and stole something that would never return.

After the boating accident I unraveled. Parts of my heart drowned in those waters that day. Not being able to envision a happy tomorrow became a part of my own death process.

There is hope, though. When we feel powerless, that is the

start of an authentic spiritual journey. When death shows up, it is the start of new life for second chancers.

Our stories are littered with death, aren't they? Do you see it in your story, my beloved?

Death of control when cancer strikes.

Death of friendships and marriages and intact families.

Death of our values that night we paid for sex.

Death of dreams and hopes and first loves.

Death of children or the hope to have them.

Death of innocence and happy childhoods.

Death of ego, pride, and got-it-togetherness.

One of the great tragedies I come across in my counseling work is people who never recognize how death has grabbed their stories. They deny it or, worse, cover it up. Death is too frightening and final for them. So they call it a "little setback." Or a "slight hiccup." Or they minimize it and say, "It's not that bad."

But let me be frank: it's hard to throw raging parties for people who have only overcome slight hiccups or little setbacks. People who talk about dealing with nicks and bruises deserve a polite golf clap or maybe a high-five. Perhaps we will get together for some appetizers and pretzels after work? Perhaps. A full-out, eardrum-busting, play-that-funky-music prodigal party? Not so much.

If you're afraid to sit in the heaviness of the deaths in your story, God is willing to go slow with you. But sooner or later you must acknowledge the losses so you can move on to the next steps of his resurrection process.

You might be thinking, *Hey, Mike, all this talk about dying is kind of bumming me out.* Okay. So let me give you the best news: God doesn't leave us in death but leads us to hope—a hope that comes from knowing that our worst-case scenario has already happened.

What would you do if you knew the world you loved was coming to an end? I would tell my friends I loved them more often. I might sing louder and longer in the shower. I would stop caring so much about what people thought about me. I would take longer naps and hug more strangers and say honest things to anyone who would listen. I would forgive faster, because the hurt doesn't hurt as much when you're dead. I'd stop listening to the critics and not be so angry when things didn't go my way. I would start pursuing my dreams, paint my first painting, and take salsa lessons on Tuesday nights and not worry about looking too stupid. Life would be crazy good.

Once you've survived something with tenacity, courage, and friends, you're free to turn your mourning into dancing. Or as poet Angela Morgan wrote:

> Be jubilant, be jubilant, O my soul,
> For thou art alive to the whole![2]

And "the whole" involves acceptance of both death and life. Graveclothes and party outfits. Don't be afraid to wear both in your story. Irreplaceable loss and sacred blessings. At Jesus's feet we are both dead and alive. Both states are required for finding wholeness.

Paul Young, author of *The Shack,* shared this in a talk he gave a couple of years ago: "There is nothing so broken in you that God doesn't know how to heal it. There is nothing so lost that he doesn't know where to find it. And nothing so dead that he can't grow something inside of it."[3] I find hope in these words. I have found them to be true in my own life.

So to understand who we are and where our lives are heading, we need more moments like the one described in my all-time favorite Bible story: the parable of the prodigal son. It's a perfect picture of the type of deaths I'm writing about and of the truth that death unleashes every reason to party. It is the story of God's calling us home to a new life.

AN ABSOLUTE FESTIVAL OF DEATH FOR LIFE

You may have heard this story before. It's a good one. It's popular. But we make a mistake in how we treat the parable. We read it as if it were one of those Sunday school children's stories, when in actuality it's a *Game of Thrones,* bloody resurrection tale. Like the gritty, shocking, and jaw-dropping plot twists of HBO's finest show, the story Jesus unpacks should have everyone talking about it the next morning. You see, the story of a wayward son and a love-crazed father is not just a welcome-home story but the outline of God's death process that leads to celebrating wholeness.

The prodigal son story is what writer Robert Farrar Capon called "an absolute festival of death."[4] Of life being taken and given and lost. The death of personal ideals and morals. Toothpaste-squirting moments, in other words. Within this parable is the utter collapse of a son's dignity and a father's obedience to society's rules.

It also demonstrates how quickly death can reduce all of life to just a few key principles. It strips away all the spiritual shenanigans and gets us to the core of what a relationship with God really looks like.

Warren Zevon, the great folk singer, went on the *Late Show with David Letterman* for what would be his last public appearance. He had lung cancer and had only two months to live. Dave asked him if his condition had taught him anything about life and death. Zevon replied, "Enjoy every sandwich."[5] Death radically focuses everything. It can be a gift if you're willing to embrace it.

In the prodigal story, Jesus reveals how we must get rid of

every ego-driven trinket and spiritual-performance award. He explains that salvation comes through our own grisly death and resurrection. This parable makes clear that all must die in order to live. Even the death of God. Let me explain.

Jesus shares how one day the younger son comes to the father and asks for his inheritance (Luke 15:12). Now, Junior is not asking Pops to cash out his trust fund early. This is not a simple request for cash but rather a backhanded request to take his father's life.

In that culture, society had stringent rules about how children obtained their inheritance. The protocol said someone had to die first. These were the rules. So the son is saying, "Hey, Dad, I want your cash but not you. So write the check and drop dead." It is a suicide request from a son who is so morally bankrupt that he places no value on the life of another or even on his own life for that matter.

After hearing the death request from the son, the listeners to Jesus's story would have been outraged by the son's utter gall. They would have thought, *Slap the boy! Disown the scumbag! Cut him off completely.* The spoiled brat has shown all his cards and revealed the heart of darkness that the dad probably knew had always been there. *Strike him down now.*

But in the story the father does something different, something shocking. He says to the son, "Yes, I will do it. I will take my life for you." He absorbs the shame of his son's request. The father endures the pain of his son's abandonment and betrayal. His life is over. Dead dad walking.

And then the prodigal son takes off and goes someplace the father could never go. A foreign land. An unclean place. Atlantic City comes to mind.

We can only imagine what he did when he got there. Jesus doesn't fill in the exact details of what happened but only says,

"He wasted all his money in wild living" (verse 13). But clearly this is his time to live it up and burn it down. Every dreamed-of sensual indulgence comes true. Hedonism on steroids. Complete, no-holds-barred freedom. He devours every type of sex, joyride, and titillation he wants. High-class hookers and ten-thousand-dollar bottle service at the club.

But as with every episode of VH1's *Behind the Music,* eventually the money runs out and the music ends. The prodigal son finds out that nobody loves you when you're a hung-over shell of a man, morally busted, with empty pockets. He falls into the dregs of shame, losing all dignity, his very identity. Everything is lost, and every scrap of self-worth and respect has disappeared.

Then, while lying in a pigsty, drooling over the slop the animals are feeding on, he realizes something. Even the guys who work for his dad have it better than this. He can't go home as a son (that toothpaste is out of the tube), but maybe he can go home and live as a servant. The son who was once tucked into bed at night by the father, the son who dined at the family table, the son who was the apple of his father's eye had died. The only hope now was to live as a servant.

So he works up a speech. A eulogy, really. One that says, "I screwed up. I know I hurt you. I ruined everything. I am a disaster. I'm not worthy to be your son. In fact, your son is dead, because I killed him when I left. And your blood is on my hands too. Please make me your servant. I don't want much. Just enough to survive. You don't even have to know my name. I'm just a worker now and will remain in the shadows of your world."

Here comes the best part. Don't miss this. It is the epic grace picture Jesus wants forever etched in your mind and tattooed on your soul. This is what he wants you to know when your life hits rock bottom and you, too, are dead inside.

When you wonder how God feels about all your outrageous

requests, and when you rehearse your speech about how you screwed it all up, and when you try to cobble a résumé to explain why he should let you be a servant, and when your shame suffocates you and your self-respect is dying a slow death, God always says, "Come home now."

THE LONGEST WALK OF SHAME

And so the son returns. He reeks of cigarettes, pigsty, and cheap hooker perfume. I'm sure it was the longest walk of shame in the history of humanity. The story says that while the son was a long way off, the father saw him and . . .

Turned away in disgusted pain?

Fired off a volley of judgment missiles?

Sent some handlers to clean him up and bring him in the back way?

No.

The father ran to the son. He stinkin' ran!

You have to understand that men in that day did not run. Absolutely not! It was considered shameful, because to do so they had to hoist up their robes and show their ankles. It would be like you or me running naked down the street. Or at the very least jogging in our underwear. Society has rules. No running naked. No showing your ankles.

But, hey, the father was as good as dead to everyone. And when you're dead to your friends, community, and family, you just don't care about certain things anymore. Every sense of social demeanor, self-respect, or proper custom was now abolished. Dad had nothing to lose. Dead man was running.

He ran.

And ran.

And ran. As fast as he could.

A lovesick, dignity-shunning stampede of grace. An out-of-control freight train of radical acceptance. He ran. He streaked. He wrapped his dead son up in his arms. He kissed his sin-caked cheeks. He wept and howled and nearly choked on his happiness.

The son was floored. He started to blurt out his eulogy, the one he'd been practicing over and over on the long journey home. "I've sinned. I'm unworthy. I'm dead as a son."

But the son never finished his speech because his father had other plans and was in no mood for silly speeches. There was no time for penance or purgatory, only prodigal parties.

Perhaps the greatest lesson for all of us second chancers is that there is never a need to explain anything at all. No excuses. No shame. No blame. No need to throw anyone under the bus, including ourselves. Just come home, God says, and forget this ridiculous idea of living as a servant.

Why did the father do this in the story? It is because the father didn't want a slave or servant. He wanted a child. He wasn't accepting applications for servants. He was only filling out adoption papers for wayward kids who did everything wrong.

And God does the same today. He's adopting sons and daughters whose names were once in the obituary section of the newspaper. Kids like you and me.

You are not a scoundrel. You are not a slave. You are a son. You are a daughter. You don't have anything more to prove. No debts left to pay. God has thrown his arms around you. His ring is proudly on your finger. The party is underway, and only those who truly know they are dead can come in.

the moment we
SAY the words
"I need HELP"
we DISMANTLE THE
SYSTEMS OF SHAME
and FEAR

MIKE FOSTER

Three

Dead Man's Party

One of the great pleasures of my life is leading an organization that is dedicated to helping people find meaning in their story of struggle. I am the founder and chief chance officer of a nonprofit called People of the Second Chance. I love what I get to do and whom I get to do it with.

I see the role we play in the world as both cheerleader and healer. We have a thriving community of second chancers who are bravely living out their stories. Through the power of social media, films, written words, and community, we have joined our voices together to amplify hope in the world.

People ask me all the time what People of the Second Chance is all about. We do a lot of different things. It's a combo of inspiration and application. I like to think of our little nonprofit as a grace-flavored snow cone on a hot judgmental day. We are helping second chancers live a better story and walking alongside them when they struggle.

A couple of years ago we launched a successful group curriculum called *Freeway: A Not-So-Perfect Guide to Freedom.*

It takes people through six steps to help them forgive and be free. I also train leaders in how to counsel hurting people at our Rescue Lab workshops, and I have created several e-courses to help people love their life again.

Our organization is currently working in more than eighty prisons across America, facilitating community groups where male, female, and juvenile inmates connect to their true identities as the beloved. It is truly rewarding work. You see, one of my big, hairy, audacious goals is to help turn our punitive society into a restorative society. We have decided that a great place to start is by reimaging America's prison system. (More on this in a moment.)

We help people deal with their many unspoken questions about their pain and loss. I think Rainer Maria Rilke captured what we point people toward when he wrote:

> Have patience with everything unresolved in your heart and . . . try to love *the questions themselves* as if they were locked rooms or books written in a very foreign language. Don't search for the answers, which could not be given to you now, because you would not be able to live them. And the point is, to live everything. *Live* the questions now. Perhaps then, someday far in the future, you will gradually, without even noticing it, live your way into the answer.[1]

Our broken lives bring so many questions and so few answers. So the point of our imperfectionist tribe is to help all of us have the patience to live out the questions and not get tripped up by them. We put forth a manifesto to enjoy the possibility of what today brings. We champion people to grab hold of their lives, no matter what condition they are in, and live boldly. Our message is this: don't miss the miracle of the now.

Every day is a chance to find meaningful ways to put love back into the world. It's not about all those pain-induced questions per se. It's about living a life that matters. And as we live, God guides us into the right answers.

What I have found in my own story of brokenness is that the first answer is to find awesome ways to love one another. Be bold with who you love. Each of us has permission to be extravagant in the encouragement of others. It makes God happy too.

One of the ways we do this in our second-chance community is by celebrating inmates, addicts, and prodigals who are finding their way back home. People like my friend Heavy.

WHEN YOU'RE HEAVY

Heavy just finished serving a thirteen-year sentence for armed robbery. He is a musclebound giant of a man with tats inked all over his body. He is thirty-seven years old and currently lives in a halfway house for parolees.

Heavy has little family support. He has one set of clothes. One pair of underwear. He recently found a job, but they sent him home the first day because he didn't have slip-resistant shoes. He can't afford the shoes because he doesn't have any money, but he can't make any money because he doesn't have shoes. It is a vicious cycle of hopelessness that many ex-felons deal with daily. They are labeled, and the odds are never in their favor. America currently operates under a penal system where 67.5 percent of the inmates who come out of prison will be rearrested within three years.[2]

The system is rigged for Heavy to fail. Plain and simple. It is one of the greatest sins of our nation.

I believe God cares deeply about injustice. I believe God's heart is close to the prisoner. In fact, according to Matthew 25:31–46 and the parable of the sheep and the goats, "the least of these" might be his number-one priority.

I imagine my first conversation with God when I get to heaven going like this:

"Hey, Mike!"

"Hey, God! Wow! This place is really, really sweet!"

"Yes, um, I know. That's why we call it heaven, Mike."

I get the official road map and adjust my halo. Then God begins to address his one-and-only topic at hand. "So listen, Mike. I loved the ministry stuff and the speaking stuff and how you worked so hard to get to church on time. And, boy, you really kicked those morning quiet times into high gear. Whole nutha level, my friend!"

"Thanks, God! I really tried my best. I'm so glad you noticed."

"That stuff was cool, but I want to ask you one really important question."

"Sure, God! What is it?"

"You know that gangbanger in prison and the lonely widow and that homeless guy sleeping in his urine-soaked jeans that you saw on the street. You know those guys?"

"Um, sure, I think I know who you're talking about," I say as I see tears forming in God's eyes.

"What did you do for the least of these? How did you love them?"

I want to have a good answer on that day. My work with prisoners and ex-cons is part of that. A big part.

Scott Larson is the chairman of Reclaiming Youth International. He serves in four hundred juvenile detention centers, where he helps high-risk youth through mentoring programs. He said:

> The prison system is an example of a massive system that has a host of complex subsystems within it—legal,

> political, economic, family, community, legislative, media, racial, and socioeconomic, to name a few. These all intersect and contribute to a mammoth system that houses more than 2.4 million people in the United States. . . . No one working in corrections or any of its subsystems would say—or even believe—they are trying to keep people coming back to prison. And yet, when more than two out of three released prisoners return within three years, one must at least become curious as to why.[3]

Jerome Miller, a pioneer in juvenile justice reform, said, "Incremental change doesn't yield anything. It's only when you change the script, the very way by which you look at the problem, that transformation can begin to happen."[4]

I am not foolish enough to believe I have all the answers, but I do want to change the script. I believe a wonderful place to start is to look at the prodigal playbook of God and his formula: death, coming to our senses, and then a party.

Sometimes audacious new ideas are quite simple. Sometimes they are more complex. I believe movements are really just made up of people making moves. Opposite moves. Irrational and surprising moves. By people willing to risk doing it differently and trying something else.

Societal shifts always involve changing the narrative from "This is the way we've always done it" to "How about we try something else?" It is having the courage to say, "This isn't working. This is not right." It means you and I being ready to ask a better question of our society.

A second chance is not just a fluffy religious concept but a provocative, life-changing idea that transforms not only our own lives but also our most broken institutional systems.

I believe that when we offer dignity and respect to those who do not deserve it—people like Heavy—a door opens to fresh possibilities. When God's beloved call out the inherent value within the marginalized, a societal, spiritual, emotional, and psychological shift happens.

Am I overreaching here? Have I lost touch with reality? Let me share a quick story.

GULAG TO GATELESS

Thirty years ago Finland's prisons had been modeled after the horrendous incarceration systems of neighboring Russia. The vicious and punitive nature of these correctional facilities produced atrocious results. Finland's penal system was as broken as the current version in America. The Finns believed it was time for a new vision, and they started making some different moves.

The country began to transition their oppressive, gulag-like prison systems into restorative treatment programs. They replaced glum cells with facilities that resemble college dormitories. They removed walls, bars, and gates and replaced them with video surveillance.

The prison staff and leadership began to treat inmates like human beings and not like caged animals. Inmates and guards address each other by their first names. Prisoners are often called "clients," and they are granted generous home leaves as their sentences near the end. Prison staff grant a new level of humanity and dignity to those who committed crimes.

The results? Today Finland, which once had one of the highest rates of incarceration, has one of the lowest in the European Union. Crime rates have dropped dramatically, and some forty thousand Finns have been spared prison. Tens of millions of dollars have been saved. It took great courage to make this shift, but the results are undeniable.[5]

And the Finns are not the only ones seeing the benefits of a different approach to incarceration. A recent Dutch newspaper article reported that the Netherlands had closed nineteen prisons last year and will shutter another five in the upcoming years. Shorter and more appropriate prison sentences, combined with a decline in the rate of serious crimes, has left thousands of prison cells empty.[6]

BECOMING PRODIGAL PARTY PLANNERS

At People of the Second Chance, we believe the status quo for the treatment of criminals in the United States is far from the best we can do. So when we met Heavy at the halfway house, we wanted to change the script for him. We decided to take a page from the prodigal son story.

After talking to him and listening to his story, we asked Heavy if we could throw a party in his honor: chicken, mac 'n' cheese, chips and salsa. A celebration of Heavy.

We made our case. "Listen, Heavy, you look like you need a good party. We think some unconditional love from people who believe in you and some nachos might help."

He responded in disbelief. "You would do that for me? A party just for me?"

"Yes, of course! How about it? You in?"

And for the first time in a long time, a hardened, musclebound hustler began to smile. Love was getting in through the cracks. The dead were being resurrected.

We invited our friends—folks from church and of course our People of the Second Chance community. We reached out to officials from the justice system and ex-cons who had turned their lives around. Heavy's pastor showed up, and one of Heavy's cousins, whom Heavy was trying to keep from making the same mistakes he had made.

My friend Margaret baked her famous white cake with white frosting. We blew up balloons and designed a big sign that read "You Rock, Heavy!" We decorated the room with streamers and red balloons and picked up some soda pop at the local supermarket.

We purchased a few small gifts for Heavy and those slip-resistant shoes he needed. And most of all we prayed that through our prodigal party God would remind Heavy that he is loved.

I asked Heavy to share his dreams with everyone. He talked about wanting to be a writer and how he wrote seventeen books in prison. He told everyone how he sometimes feels judged because of his size, his tattoos, and the color of his skin. Heavy talked about how, when he was growing up, getting good grades and writing stories was frowned upon in the projects of the inner city. He quickly learned the rules of the street. He figured out fast that it was easier to survive as a street hustler than as a writer.

After he finished sharing, he pulled me aside and said, "You know what, Mike? That was the first time in my life that I felt like anybody has actually ever listened to me."

That night we celebrated a felon who needed a party. We watched an ex-con find hope. Fellow prodigals shared their own stories to help Heavy be not so heavy. We were a fellowship of wounded warriors.

This concept is so simple that we now invite others in our community to join the parties these days. We believe everyone plays a part in creating these celebrations. It is so much fun to join the work of the kingdom by welcoming prodigals home. I think you should try it too.

Social activist Abbie Hoffman said, "The only way to support a revolution is to make your own."[7] Right now, all across the country, prodigal parties are popping up. Fiestas are bubbling up in unlikely places. I'm attending one next week.

Why is this idea catching on? There are two basic reasons.

The first reason is that everybody knows somebody who needs a party. Can you think of someone right now? I bet you can.

All of us have someone in our lives who needs to be reminded that he or she is loved. There are a lot of Heavys out there. You have them in your neighborhood, workplace, maybe even your own family. Just find your Heavy.

There are people who are dead and need resurrection—friends, strangers, classmates, couples, preachers, and single moms who have come to the end of themselves and want to quit. If you can't think of at least one name right now, I beg you to go for a walk in your neighborhood. Open your eyes and look around. Go to AA meetings or convalescent homes, or check your Facebook page.

Check in the thin cracks of our society. Look behind the 7-Eleven trash bins or at the bus stop. Find someone who needs a party. Trust me, they are out there.

The second reason the prodigal party idea is catching on is that everybody knows what a party is and how to do one.

Isn't that fantastic?! Everyone is prequalified. You don't have to go to college or pay for some online course to throw a party. The know-how is already there.

I love how the father in the parable of the prodigal son used what was already on hand. No need to go grocery shopping or make a Costco run. He just dove right into party mode with the available resources.

Fatted calf? Check.

Family ring? Check.

Fine robe? Check.

Sandals? Check.

Older brother? Unchecked. Not here? Hmm.

Diet Coke? Unchecked? Hmm. Well, that's too bad. We party anyway. The dead have come back home, and the resurrection party can't wait. We work with what we have.

Every party can look different and reflect the needs, personality, and creativity of the party host. The only real guideline is to have fun and to celebrate the uncelebrated. The rest is up to you. Unleash your creative, artistic, and visionary gifts. Let freedom reign, and do whatever moves you. Prodigals aren't picky.

I also love that parties can happen anywhere. Location options are endless. They happen in second chancers' homes and backyards. Sometimes at burger joints or church fellowship halls. Maybe in the lunchroom at the office or the local Panera Bread.

My friend Jeff Conway owns a Ruth's Chris Steak House. Once a year he goes into the Clarksville Correctional Facility in South Carolina and hosts his own version of a prodigal party.

Inside the correctional facility Jeff sets up an official Ruth's Chris Steak House experience. White tablecloths. Beautifully folded napkins. He brings his staff and his shining silverware and his spotless wineglasses from the restaurant. And then they party. He serves filet mignon, jumbo shrimp, Caesar salads, and cheesecake for dessert. He gives the inmates five-star service and serves up a good portion of honor and respect. They are treated just as if they were in his restaurant.

Jeff understands the power of a party to transform lives. He brings radical love by serving dignity one jumbo shrimp at a time.

PARTY FOR THE DEAD

I attended a funeral a few weeks ago. It was a lovely ceremony with Scripture reading, funny family stories, and a photomontage.

Afterward we made our way out of the chapel to a small reception hosted in the fellowship hall. Sugar cookies and punch were served. Instrumental organ music played in the background. People talked quietly and respectfully. This is how most Americans do funeral receptions.

But perhaps this is a muted picture of how we should respond to mortality. If we actually understood the true dynamics of life and death, maybe our response would be different. The ending of life is a somber thing but also a reason for a party.

Jesus seems to be pointing out in the prodigal son story that we need to be dead men to get into his parties. It is why the older brother stayed outside. He wasn't dead yet. The father and wayward son were. Death sets the pace for the party.

Heavy died in a prison cell as a result of the crime he committed and having his human dignity stripped away while incarcerated. When we celebrated him, we needed to party hard. Prodigal parties should look more like a spirited Irish wake or a Ghanaian funeral celebration. Let me explain.

Sam Dolnick, in a *New York Times* article about funerals in Ghana, paints a stark contrast with our typical subdued American funeral reception. He says this of what could only be described as over-the-top Ghanaian funerals: "They are all-night affairs with open bars and window-rattling music. . . . Disc jockeys, photographers, videographers, bartenders and security guards—keep it all humming." Coffins "resemble Mardi Gras floats."[8]

This is not our normal, is it? This response to death feels odd to Western culture. It might feel inappropriate or even offend you. You might struggle with the idea of dancing the Macarena at grandma's funeral. And, honestly, a prodigal party that celebrates felons should feel odd too. It is weird. It is abnormal. It's backward, right?

You might be struggling with these questions:

1. What about the victims?
2. How will guys like Heavy ever learn their lesson?
3. Why spend all this time and money that could go toward something else?

I understand all those questions and have wrestled with them myself. I would never want to be insensitive to the victims of crime or overlook our society's laws. In my work I have spent many years in the trenches with all types of victims. I have cried many tears and consoled those who have been deeply wronged by another individual. I have also watched firsthand as the power of forgiveness transformed a victim's life. Sadly, I have also watched unforgiveness poison those who have been wronged, making it impossible for them to find real freedom. Either way, the choice belongs to the person who has been harmed.

The true beauty of God's relationship with us is that he allows us to choose our response to scandalous grace. He asks us to trust him. He asks us to surrender control. He invites us into opposite living and a lifestyle that often looks, according to our cultural norms, irresponsible, reckless, and scandalous.

I promise, the act of forgiveness will turn your stomach sometimes. The decision to release others from the harm they have caused is inherently unfair. Second chances often fly in the face of common decency. It is scandalous. But the scandal seeks freedom for both the oppressed and the oppressor. The focus is freedom and expansion of life no matter how nauseating it might feel at first. Second-chance living requires doing things that buck our society's rules and at times our sense of common decency.

You see, my fellow second chancer, we desire to radically change the script for people caught in a destructive downward spiral. We will never change the world by doing things that make sense. Societal and religious norms must be pushed to the brink of absurdity sometimes in order to move us forward. Setting up a

Ruth's Chris Steak House inside a prison and serving cheesecake for dessert? Huh? Whatcha talkin' 'bout, Willis? And this is the gloriously messy scandal of grace.

The story of the kingdom is found in a raging fiesta for someone who doesn't deserve one. The father says, "We had to celebrate and be glad, because this brother of yours was dead and is alive again" (Luke 15:32, NIV). The theology of grace is in the party. The gospel is in the balloons and piñatas, which is made possible only by death and resurrection. The death and resurrection of Jesus and our own death and second-chance resurrection. So let's rise and let's party.

LET'S INSPIRE EACH OTHER NOT TO BE JUST *better* HUMAN BEINGS BUT MORE *whole* HUMAN BEINGS.

MIKE FOSTER

Four

Be Brave with Your Story

It has been asked millions of times in millions of ways in millions of homes, apartments, and department stores across the world. What is this one brutally unfair question thrust upon the innocent bystander? It is this: "Does this dress make me look fat?"

It comes to us in many different flavors. The word *dress* may be swapped for the names of other garments, such as jeans, shirts, and bathing suits. The question may be set up in a different manner as well. It may come out as "These pants make me look fat, don't they?" Which is really more of a statement than a question. A declaration of war with no diplomacy. Now we not only have to pick a position but also defend it.

I've found this unanswerable question often pops up in a subtler way in my home. I'm standing in the bathroom with my wife, Jennifer. She is getting ready. She mumbles the question under her breath, just loud enough for me to hear it.

Now I'm trapped. I can't just ignore the question. She knows I heard it. So I can't pretend it never happened. I'm not that clever or that good at lying.

Many a person, myself included, has tried to give an answer. But in the immortal words of Admiral Gial Ackbar from *Return of the Jedi,* "It's a trap!"

The problem with the question is twofold. First, it assumes the worst. Second, it has no good answer. It contains the seeds of mutually assured destruction.

Sometimes we do this with our own stories too. We assume the worst and create questions with no good answers. Our lives are happening, and we don't like it. We believe something is inherently wrong and whatever the situations, circumstances, or trajectories, our stories are not how we imagined them to be. We feel stuck or wish for something different. Our lives are not fitting our expectations. We turn to a friend and ask the impossible question: Does my story make me look fat?

This is especially true when we look at those events in our lives that obviously took a turn for the worse. We begin to ask others:

"Does my past addiction make me look irresponsible?"

"Does my divorce make me damaged goods?"

"Does my bankrupted business mean I'm not a good leader?"

"Does my eating disorder disqualify me from now being into health and fitness?"

Sometimes our stories fit like a favorite pair of jeans. Perfect, effortless, wonderful. We're rocking those babies. Then there are other parts of our story that feel like those jeans have been baked in the dryer at superhigh heat and shrunk three sizes. We can still pull them on, but just barely. We can't button the top buttons. Our fat oozes over the waistband with muffin tops and beer bellies hanging onto the edge for dear life. We can barely bend or breathe. Rather than our rocking the jeans, they rock us. And we'd rather not leave the house, or we'd at least like to avoid a full-length mirror if at all possible.

As second chancers, we need to see our stories as if they're our clothes. Sometimes what's happened in our stories fits perfectly. Sometimes we have to grow into them over time. Maybe they're like those rainbow flip-flops or the fluorescent-blue Hawaiian shirt. They look great at a tropical luau but might not make sense at a friend's wedding. Certainly our stories make better sense in some contexts, but no matter what we are wearing, we gotta rock it loud and proud.

When God writes our lives, there are never mistakes, just movements to bring us closer to him. He writes stories of love and messiness that connect us to one another. God's narrative always gets you and me closer to embodying love and releasing all the beauty inside us.

So we should never be ashamed of how our story fits. We should never hide the words, characters, scenes, and cliff-hangers that make up our stories of grace. We rob each other of sacred friendship when we delete moments, erase characters, or censor the scandalous parts. But when we share them honestly, we help others breathe easier about whatever stories they have inside. I think this is success in life. These are holy moments.

A STORY IN PROCESS

For most of my life, I have shared my story. I speak and I write. I tweet and I Instagram. I have grown comfortable sharing my struggles. I have come to see how my broken parts matter. This is my spirituality on display.

In general, I do my best to make sure I don't look that good. It's not a self-hatred thing. Just my best understanding of how life should be lived and my deep conviction of how we should interact with each other. People may be drawn to confidence, but they connect with weakness. I've grown skeptical of people who are the heroes in every story. So I think about ways to authentically share my weak moments. With friends. In presentations. On social media. With my kids. I want to be seen not as a hero but instead as a wounded warrior. It fits me better, and it's a lot more fun.

My life is still a work in process, as is yours. It is true that I am both the doctor and the patient. A wonderful remix of contradictions and clarity. Sometimes I rock my jeans, and sometimes my jeans rock me.

I must confess it is an odd predicament when a book publisher asks you to write down your thoughts about second chances and grace. Then the publisher says to the reader, "Listen to this guy. He knows some stuff. His words are important."

And I think, *But don't they know me? Don't they see my hypocrisy and lies? My stupid moments and ridiculous failures and overwhelming insecurities? Haven't they Googled me? For heaven's sake, people, Google me before you ask me to write a book that's supposed to help someone.*

Don't they know that some people out there wonder if I'm even a Christian? Don't they know I yell at my kids for doing stupid kid stuff and love to whine when Chipotle doesn't put enough guacamole in my burrito? Shouldn't they be aware that I am prone to want to drink a whole bottle of wine when I'm sad and sometimes love football on Sunday mornings more than church? It's all true. I promise.

I am a hot mess with a hopeful message. It is a message of self-compassion, forgiveness, and loving the unlovable parts of us. I'm not an expert but rather an equal, and together we are learning to tell our second-chance stories. If we can do this, we will heal hurting hearts: our hearts and our friends' hearts.

And though I have lived as openly as I can, there are still parts of my story that are hard for me to say out loud. Honestly, I've been a little chicken. Or at least a little rooster who cock-a-doodle-doos really quietly about certain parts of who I am.

I have things in my story where words and explanations don't make sense to me, so how could they ever make sense to anyone willing to listen? It has been hard to believe that the painful parts of my story actually fit on me. They look funny and fat and weird, and it's hard to describe them when I see them on me. So I have kept quiet.

Can you relate? Have you ever thought, *Why bother?* Why bring that old, stale hurt back into the light? It's easier to stay silent. That is the safest way to avoid misunderstanding and misrepresentation. I'd rather they not know. So we say nothing. Our stories are unspoken.

But as author Zora Neale Hurston pointed out, "There is no agony like bearing an untold story inside you."[1] She's right you know.

I am proposing a movement where we say the things that others deem shameful and worthless. I believe grace has a voice and that voice is ours. It comes in the form of things we're not supposed to say. The imperfectionist movement begins with individuals being courageous with their words and stories, feeling safe to speak the unspeakable things. What the Enemy meant to be a curse can now flow out of our mouths as a blessing. You and I become heroes with our words when we fearlessly speak the truth of who we are, what we've done, and who we are becoming.

THE CHORUS OF FROGS

Spadefoot toads live all over the American West. They gather in large groups around ponds and vernal pools. When they gather, they sing together. They pulsate and vocalize in unison, creating a harmonious toad song.

Spadefoot toads do this for two reasons. One is for mating. The other is for protection. As they create a unified choir, it makes it difficult for predators, such as foxes, coyotes, and owls, to come in and pick off any individual toad. Their song saves them. Their synchronicity brings protection.[2]

The same is true of second chancers. We must collectively lock our vulnerable stories together. Create a choir that gladly sings about our brokenness and how we are not perfect but are perfectly loved. If you don't know the words of your second-chance story yet, don't worry. We can just hum a song together.

There is strength and safety in numbers. We must never forget that we are not alone. Kurt Vonnegut, in a letter to a friend, wrote, "Most people don't have good gangs, so they are doomed to cowardice."[3]

We need not be afraid. We have each other and a God who is for us. I've heard it said that the most common one-liner in the Bible is "Do not be afraid." Someone supposedly counted and said it shows up 365 times, once for each day of the year. Others say that the phrase appears more frequently than that. Either way, if you're like me, we need more than one "Do not be afraid" per day.

I also want us to create a world where you and I have a community of friends who will listen compassionately to our not-so-perfect stories. When we say scary things and weird stuff, they will understand. Not judge us. Not roll their eyes. Not say things that make us feel even weirder about the story we wear. Friends who will listen to us and not try to fix us.

Mr. Rogers said, "The purpose of life is to listen—to yourself, to your neighbor, to your world and to God and, when the time comes, to respond in as helpful a way as you can find . . . from within and without."[4] I think that's a good purpose for all of us who are trying to live in hope and grace.

How about I go first with my hard-to-say story, and then you can think of your story after I'm done? Okay? So deep breath. Here we go.

THE STORY I'M AFRAID TO SHARE

It's hard to know where to start. The words are unrehearsed and have been hidden in my heart for so long. I can count on one hand the number of people I have discussed this with, and even that was only in short conversations. I did not want to bother them so much with this part of my story.

As a child I visited an older widow who was part of my extended family. Usually in the summertime and a few weekends a year, my parents dropped me off to spend a few days with her in Los Angeles.

Her property was in constant disarray. To call her lawn a lawn would be a bit of a stretch. But I worked in her yard. Pulled weeds. Mowed over the dried-out spots that checkered her lawn. I didn't have to be good at landscaping, because whatever meager stuff I did unquestionably improved the condition of her yard. The mower roared over rocks and sticks and dried grass, engulfing me in a tornado cloud of dust and specks of fescue.

She let me play with stick matches, and I would light an entire box in one day. The magic of creating a spark of fire was remarkable to a ten-year-old. I would often light a single pine needle and get the tip glowing and smoking, then pretend I was taking a hit on a cigarette. I thought I was cool.

I wasn't cool, but with a pine-needle cigarette in my hand and a box full of matches, I felt invincible.

In the evenings she would prepare fried chicken and potatoes, and I would drink Dr Pepper. Her house was cluttered with trinkets and old china. Black-and-white family photos, along with empty bottles of perfume, covered every surface.

At night she brought me into her bed. She didn't want me to sleep in the other room. She had a queen-size feather bed with fluffy pillows.

When we were in bed together, she asked me to touch her. Sexually. She placed my hands under her loose, muumuu nightgown and instructed me to caress her in different places. She would only stroke my cheek and nothing more. The only sound was the creaking of the bed and a radio playing the news of the day.

I never understood why this happened every evening. I just knew she expected it. Today I know it was molestation. I know it was wrong. No young boy should have to do those things. Ever.

It was confusing for a boy to be directed to do such horrible things in the dark of night and then to wake up in the morning and enjoy the best flapjacks and maple syrup he'd ever had. How is a boy supposed to process the inputs of delicious fried chicken, smoking pine-needle cigarettes, hopeless lawn maintenance, and being forced to fondle an older woman?

The reality of these nights has been a part of my secret story for decades. It's something I feel embarrassed about. It's hard to get the words out about this part of my life. The threat of misunderstanding, of losing control is palpable. The story hovers over my shoulder with a battle-ax of shame, ready to crash down on me.

But I won't bow to shame. I won't refuse to share, because this really happened. It's truth. And I'm not scared anymore.

THE LIES THAT TRAP OUR STORIES

In the silence that ensued when I chose not to talk about my molestation, lies began to grow in my mind. I want to tell you about a couple of the big lies I began to think were true about this experience. I think for many of us they can be huge barriers in telling others about what we've been through.

Lie 1: It wasn't a big deal.

This is one of the most common lies we tell ourselves when something bad has happened to us. We survived it. It was a long time ago. We moved on. We lead semihappy lives and eat at Chick-fil-A a couple times a week, so it must not have been that big a deal.

After an event like sexual molestation or any childhood trauma, we try to seal it in our heads. If we can bury it deep in our memories, then it's fixed, we think. Dan Allender, in his book *The Wounded Heart,* says that a "sexually abused person often denies the abuse, mislabels it, or at least minimizes the damage."[5] It is how we protect our hearts and cope with such things. But it's not that simple, is it?

You cannot bury a wound. No matter how far you push it back or how much denial you pile on top of it, the wound remains. Want proof? When you think about that event, does it make you want to throw up? Does it feel like a dark cloud has just passed over your heart? I still shiver about those summers even though it happened three decades ago.

Here's another test: Are there certain stories you can't listen to? It's hard for me to watch news stories where teachers or older women have sexual contact with teen or preteen boys. The dialogue seems to revolve around the women's good looks and snide remarks about how the boys probably loved it. "Those boys got lucky" is the sentiment, suggesting to me that this molestation fulfilled some twisted fantasy for the reporters, viewers, and commentators.

As a child who had sexual contact with a much older female, I can adamantly state it wasn't a fantasy. What she did was distorted, crossing a sacred boundary between an adult and a child. But boys who go through things like this are faced with a dilemma. The tabloid-media types and shock bloggers rear their haughty heads and imply that we're supposed to consider our sexual experiences as a conquest, an initiation into manhood. A subtle shaming occurs, a notion that we should feel lucky or privileged by unwanted sexual touch, so the victim stays quiet, perplexed by how his disgust or confusion fits into the story.

So let me be clear. If you experienced molestation as a child, whether you were a girl or a boy, whether your abuser was of the same sex or the opposite sex, whether the abuser was old or young, what you went through was a violation. It was wrong. You should not bury it. You should not accept it. You should bring it into the light.

The same goes for all the tragedies and injustice we've suffered that we're tempted to downplay. Minimizing is an effective coping mechanism for our pain but is never the pathway to true healing.

Lie 2: I will be defined by my secret shame.

I debated with myself *a lot* about whether to share this story in this book. I second-guessed myself out of my own insecurity. But I've tried to live by what Brené Brown said in her book *Rising Strong*: "The irony is that we attempt to disown our difficult stories to appear more whole or more acceptable, but our wholeness—even our wholeheartedness—actually depends on the integration of all of our experiences, including the falls."[6] Everyone wants to look whole and okay. The fear is that if we share our stories, the image we have so carefully constructed over the years will crumble. Yet the opposite is true. In our vulnerability we are building something holy.

Everyone who shares difficult stories wonders if he or she will be misunderstood. But because of the sexual nature of my story, I know certain conversations will follow. That is the bigger concern when you and I share the difficult stuff. We are tempted to believe that the painful parts of our story will become our only story, that we'll be defined solely by our trauma.

I am fine talking about my boat accident and other bad moments in my past. Those are parts of my narrative I feel safe talking about. Even when it's hard to admit these failures and setbacks, I know that good flows from my words and has the potential to heal hearts, including mine.

But this story? That young boy lying in that feather bed? It felt like too much. I feared that this story would define our conversation. That it would define *me.*

And that's how we all feel when we think about revealing our most vulnerable moments. We wonder, *Is this what I will be known for now?*

Abuse and childhood trauma in any category can bring such a definitive mark to conversations. Does this mean other men will want to speak to me about their molestation? Will I be pigeonholed as a victim? A survivor? Damaged goods?

The fear in bringing old wounds to light is that others will start to view us only through the lens of our past. That we will be forever labeled with our most tragic memory. But that is a lie. We are so much more than one awful story. Our past is not something that holds us back or defines us. It's simply a part of who we are. A dimension of what God is making us into.

YOU ARE NOT YOUR PAST

I am not my boating accident nor my weaknesses nor those summer evenings in a bed when I was a boy. I am all of it, just as you are the sum of your experiences. But our fears of being defined by our past pain often stand in the way of telling the truth. They keep us from saying the things we need to say.

Whatever your story looks like, you have the right to tell it and talk about it however you want. There can be parts that are sacred and that only you and God know. You should never be forced to disclose them. But I do invite you into a new place of freedom where you don't have to be scared to say what you need to say. You don't have to fear rejection, and you are not defined by any single event in your past.

Some people won't understand, and I'm sure a few will say things that make you wish you had been less brave. But I still want you to be a truth teller. I want you rocking the foundations of captivity and shame and all the systems that try to keep you silent.

DON'T JUDGE YOUR UNFINISHED STORY

Sometimes we don't know what to say. But other times we start to tell our story and then make the mistake of judging it while we're in the middle of it. That is like getting up in the middle of *The Lord of the Rings: The Return of the King* and giving it two thumbs down. It's like giving a one-star review to *The Sixth Sense* without seeing the ending. (Spoiler alert: Bruce Willis's character is dead.)

Don't write a critical review too early in the process. You are not a rotten tomato. Your story is still unfolding, so don't judge it too soon. Don't be like teenagers going through their first breakup, believing the world is over and they will never love again.

Also, never compare your beginning to someone else's ending. That only brings a load of discouragement. In fact, don't compare yourself to others at all. God doesn't. Why should you? Comparison only leads us to talk bad about ourselves and others. We get infected with the *I'll nevers.*

I'll never get this temptation under control.

I'll never get it right.

I'll never achieve my dreams.

I'll never feel good about my accomplishments.

and thoughts. Take a look back into the scenes of your life and begin to notice what you see. Are you scared? Are you out of control? What is being said? What is happening? When your heart begins to speak, take good notes.

2. Write the first sentence.

I have always found it to be helpful when I take the things in my head and write them down. If I take all that swirly stuff in my mind and get out a black Sharpie and jot down a few things, I can then work with them. It doesn't have to be all the details of the story. Just a simple sentence that captures the essence.

When we write the first sentence, it is like the holy, invisible, all-powerful God reducing himself to a blazing bush. Or to a cooing baby in a Bethlehem stable. The same thing happens when you courageously grab something huge in your untold story and write the truest sentence about it that you can. It is a sacred moment when you write a handful of unspoken words on a piece of paper for the first time. Ink to paper. Mystery to clarity. Captivity to freedom. Scandal to second chance.

I'm not asking you to write a book. Or a blog post. I'm not even asking you to tell your fellow second chancers yet. I only want you to write something tiny but powerful. You need a summary sentence that captures the core of what you have been too scared to say. It doesn't have to be fancy or eloquent. It just needs to be true. Don't judge the sentence. Don't water down the words. Just write what is true.

Best-selling author Cheryl Strayed was asked to give some advice on good writing. What was the key for her? She said, "I'd stopped being grandiose. I'd lowered myself to the notion that the absolute only thing that mattered was getting that extra beating heart out of my chest. . . . It was only then, when I humbly surrendered, that I was able to do the work I needed to do."[8] It is in that place of humble surrender that we will write our first sentence.

STORIES OF HOPE

The good news about your story (no matter what it looks like) is that when you have the courage to break your silence, you can be confident it will speak to the hearts of friends and strangers. It brings hope, no matter how messy the story feels or how bad it looks to you.

I think of my friends Jay and Katherine Wolf.

Seven years ago Katherine had an arteriovenous malformation that ruptured in her brain. She was twenty-six years old, a new mother with so much life to live. While staring at an old family photo, Katherine now says, "The picture looks different today."

Katherine still battles through double vision, deafness, facial paralysis, and motor-coordination issues. She uses a walker and slurs her speech. She drools when she eats.

Jay, who had been preparing to be an attorney, is now a 24/7 caregiver for Katherine. His story looks different too. They honestly admit, "God saved her life, but much has been taken away."

Despite all the things that are broken, Jay and Katherine believe our stories of suffering should bring hope to others.

Katherine says, "Hope is a powerful force. It charges us to live in the present as if we already knew the end of the story."

When we speak our imperfect stories, we are left with something real: us. You and me. Your story and mine.

When truth is spoken, it has the potential to shift our entire universe. When courageous storytellers come on the scene, the angels in heaven cheer, the winds of grace blow strong, and the bondage of shame is broken.

Your story doesn't make you look fat. It makes you *you.*

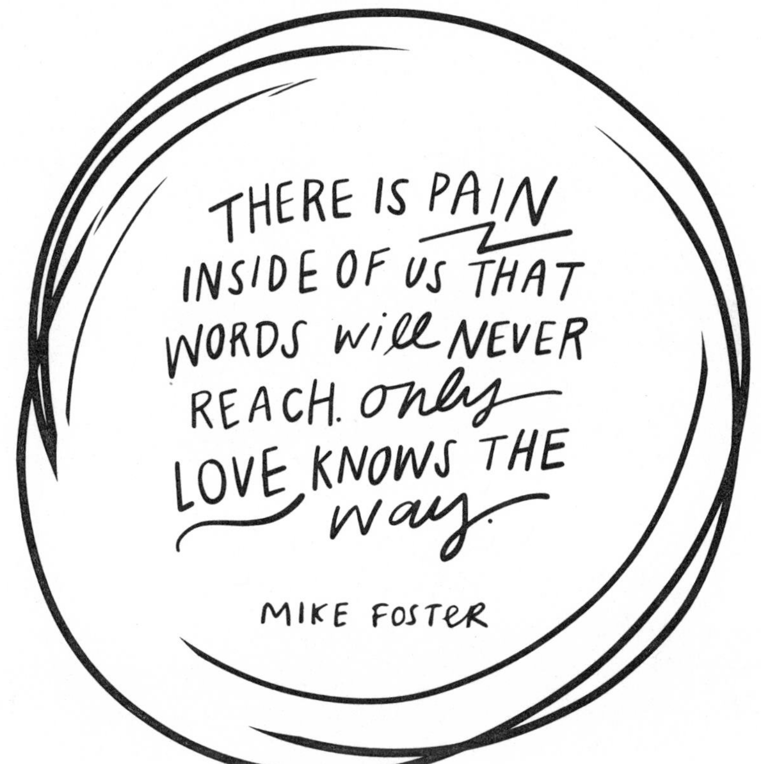
THERE IS PAIN
INSIDE OF US THAT
WORDS will NEVER
REACH. only
LOVE KNOWS THE
way.
MIKE FOSTER

Five

The Wonderful in the Weird

My friend Jon and I were cruising on a back road in Lexington, Kentucky, chatting about church that night. I had just finished speaking at Jon's church, and we were headed to a Christmas party. Jon's small group was getting together for some holiday festivities.

Jon said, "Mike, I can't wait for you to meet my friends. They are a crazy bunch. So many great stories and stuff. We always have fun getting together."

"That sounds great, Jon. Can't wait to meet everyone."

"Oh, and before I forget, I gotta tell you about Donnie."

"Okay, who's Donnie?"

"Well, Donnie is a friend of mine. Our family has kind of adopted him. And Donnie loves people, Mike. I mean, he *really* loves people. So just be ready."

My mind raced. Why did Jon feel it was necessary to prepare me for Donnie's big love?

A minute later we pulled up to the house. We walked in, and Jon led me through an unofficial meet and greet. I was the new guy. The skinny dude from California. But I can really shine in these situations. One of my strengths is schmoozing. Not sure if it's an official spiritual gift, but I have some supernatural woo inside me.

After a while Jon leaned toward me. I thought he was going to tell me to back off the enchiladas, but instead he said, "Hey, Mike. Donnie is here. You ready?"

I wasn't.

The room changed. The dynamic lifted. Donnie came in like a storm. "Merry Christmas, everyone! I'm so glad to be here," he shouted.

He wore a red sweater emblazoned with a Christmas tree and a reindeer button. His thick, black-rimmed glasses matched his ruffled black hair peppered with gray. His gray Dockers matched his Vans shoes. He bounded through the crowd giving giant hugs to everyone.

"I love you so much!" This was the declaration he announced over each friend. And by *friend* I mean *person.* Every human being there that night. Donnie did not trouble himself with categories of friend or not friend.

"I love you, I love you, I love you." He squeezed. He smiled. He meant it. Each person, one at a time, was anointed by Donnie's no-holds-barred love.

He eventually made his way to where I stood in the kitchen. There we were. Standing face to face. The moment of truth. Donnie and me.

Jon said, "Hey, Donnie, this is my friend Mike." He pointed at me with a devilish smirk on his face.

And then in a glorious moment lacking any ceremonial protocol, Donnie grabbed me and hugged me as I've never been hugged before or since. He squeezed me and patted my back. It was the fullest embrace I have ever received. It wasn't a short hug. It wasn't a long hug. It was a really, really, really long hug.

Donnie was only five feet four inches tall. I'm six foot four. Even though I stood a foot taller, it felt as if the biggest man I've ever met was wrapping me in a giant embrace, as if the arms of God had scooped me up in his unconditional, reckless love. These God-sized hugs were accompanied by kisses to my neck. Donnie stood on his tippy toes and smacked a few good ones on me. His scruffy beard and whiskers tickled my skin.

FROM WEIRD TO WONDERFUL

Part of me wants to back away from any and all weirdness. To limit my time in overwhelming moments. But over the years I've learned an important lesson. The key to a heaven-designed moment is simply to go with it. Don't mess it up. Let it be what it's going to be. Let the weird turn into wonderful.

Many of us miss out on the hugs of heaven and whispers of God's love, because he is kind of weird sometimes. He gets a kick out of surprising us and messing with our propriety and togetherness. Men don't hug like this. Strangers don't become best friends in three milliseconds. Short, bearded men aren't supposed to kiss other men's clean-shaven necks after knowing that neck for just five seconds.

The angels must slap their knees and roll with laughter when they orchestrate moments like this. When they blast us out of our comfort zones like human cannonballs.

But going with it is key. Rolling with the moment and not pushing back is pretty important if you want to turn the weird into something wonderful. God moves us into a new experience and says, "You down with this? Or do you want to cut and run?"

The spiritual life revolves around this central question: "You wanna have some fun?"

Or to put it another way, "You wanna come to a party? You wanna know my love?"

Our response makes the difference between a God-sized heart and a human-sized heart. It's the adventure of rolling with angelic invitations or saying, "Nah, that's too weird for me." It's about saying yes to God's wildness or saying yes to our own control.

Every spiritual moment that matters seems to come packaged in the befuddling overthrow of cultural norms and personal rules. God loves to wait beyond the doors we never think to walk through. He loves to love us through people we'd never choose to know.

When my story of brokenness builds an instant bridge to the hearts of strangers, I still wonder why. When I give what I don't have, more seems to conveniently show up. When I love my enemies, my life explodes in meteoric proportions and takes a giant leap forward. When I love only those who love me, the universe yawns.

The upside-down God is good at what he does. He turns weirdness into wonder. He uses opposites, prodigals, and everyday quirkiness to shame the zealous, religious know-it-alls.

God lives on the perimeters of our comfort zones. He refuses to make his way into the center of them. He invites us to take a small walk toward the outer bounds of "I'm not sure" and "I don't know" and "What's going on here?"

COME AWAY WITH ME

If we truly want to experience the richness of the second-chance life, we have to practice a little faith sometimes. We have to say a few tiny yeses to new experiences and parties and meeting new people and allowing life not to fit within a nice box. Our part is faith; God's part is surprise.

And so here I was, wrapped up in Donnie's arms. He held me and said, "I love you. I love you. I love you, Mike."

"I love you too, Donnie," I responded.

I wasn't sure what those words meant, but I had no problem saying them and feeling them. Your heart often speaks before you have the meaning of it all.

Donnie is an unlikely love cat. He grew up in an abusive home. His father was a police officer who came home from work each day and felt the need to physically vent his volcanic rage on Donnie's family. Richard Rohr said that if we don't learn how to transform our pain, we will transmit it to others.[1] Our hurts need to go somewhere. Donnie's father transmitted his pain directly to his family, creating a home of violence and cruelty that took its toll on Donnie. His dad eventually committed suicide, dealing with his demons with a bullet and a gun.

Psychologists aren't sure what happened, but something broke inside Donnie's mind. Whatever he saw, felt, or experienced froze him in a state of childhood. As Jon said, "Donnie is like a kid in a man's body." A kid who knows how to love.

That night wasn't only about hugs but also about presents. Presents that Donnie had saved all year for. At a part-time job in a fast-food pasta joint, Donnie earns $700 a month. He pays his monthly bills with $400. The other $300 is for presents. He saves each month so he can give. Generously. I did the math, and that's 43 percent of his income. He doesn't do it for tax deductions or out of abundance. Donnie gives because he *loves* to give.

He shops at garage sales and rummages through clearance racks at Wal-Mart for hot buys. He looks for specials and red-tagged items. The gifts might be dinged, outdated, or both, but that's never the point for Donnie. It's not about the gift but about the giving.

So when gift time came after dinner, Donnie beamed. This was the moment he had waited for all night. But first there would be a song. Donnie felt confident that a good way to add more joy to the festivities was to sing a worship song. He popped in a worship CD and let it rip. The song he sang at the top of his lungs, mostly out of tune, was Jesus Culture's "Come Away."

Come away with me . . .
It's not too late for you.[2]

I've never seen a man worship with more gusto and reckless abandon. Donnie brought as much passion to his singing as he did to his hugging. Hands in the air. Veins popping out on his neck. Hips swaying to the beat of the song. The melody was lost in the passion, but Donnie knew exactly what he was singing over all of us in those moments.

The lyrics were a clear invitation to join a larger party. To open our hearts to a life of expectation and possibility. To lose our fears. To lay down our worry and cynicism and release our death grip on life. To come away with the Father.

And it felt as if God was saying, "Just follow Donnie. He has the directions. He'll show you the way."

His singing voice was far from perfect, but I swear it sounded like angels. This was the best worship I was ever a part of.

After the impromptu praise jam, Donnie gathered up the gifts he wanted to give everyone. He pulled out his list of names with the corresponding gifts. You see, Donnie doesn't give random gifts. He shops with focus and intent. He sees every face and knows every name and imagines what each person might really want from the clearance bin.

For the ladies he buys jewelry. For the men he buys cologne and tools.

One of the biggest surprises of the night was that Donnie had brought a gift for me. I was blown away. *What? I'm on Donnie's gift list?* That was unreal.

I unwrapped the gift with eager anticipation but also with care. I wanted to slowly savor the moment.

Donnie had purchased a British Sterling cologne gift set for me. It was a two-for-one deal. A bottle of cologne plus a bonus aftershave lotion. I have to admit, I had never heard of British Sterling cologne up to this moment. I did some research and found that it is made by the same company that makes the slightly more popular English Leather cologne. British Sterling has what the maker describes as a "blend of warm woods, citrus, amber and moss" and is "recommended for evening wear."[3] It was the best Christmas gift ever, and I still have it today!

Hugs, gifts, and prophetic songs. Heaven came down that night. It was the party of prodigals turbocharged by the love and grace of a kid stuck in a man's body. I will never, ever forget it.

We like to seem smart, together, and with it. We like to be chosen and loved based on our talents, our gifts—the worth we have built up for ourselves. But that is not why God loves us. It's not why he loves you. That's not how you get his best.

Jesus told us that the kingdom belongs to those who are like little children (Matthew 18:3). To those who are childlike in their trust. That night I saw a living example of what that looks like. God used the foolish things of the world (a child stuck in a man's body) to show me, this wise guy, this speaker, this person trying to schmooze the room, what true joy looks like. What true love looks like.

It was a little glimpse of kingdom living I will never forget. You see, Donnie is already living in the joy, love, and peace that Jesus promises all of us. He is already living a life of complete trust. Childlike faith. No-holds-barred affection and acceptance. He is at the party.

Someday God will heal Donnie's mind and intellect. But I think his heart will require very little change. For myself and the rest of us, it's our hearts that need the work. We need to love each other more, the way Donnie loved everyone in that room. He was fluent in the language of love.

LOVE HANDLES

We talk a lot about love as a feeling. We say we love a food, a place, a sports team, a person. Usually what we mean is that it gives us certain feelings. Warm fuzzies of affection or strong bonds of preference. Donnie felt all those things, I'm sure. But it was not his feelings that made me feel so loved. It was his actions. It was what he did with those feelings that made the difference.

Sometimes we hear the command to love one another, and we're like, *Okay, I'm down with that, but how? How do I generate warm fuzzies and strong preference for the people in my life? Pray? Go to church? Anxiously await a mystical experience?*

Donnie can teach us some practical ways to love others. I call them love handles.

Reach out and touch somebody.

Touching has gotten a bad rap lately. The news is filled with stories of people abusing the power of touch, which makes us a little gun-shy when it comes to putting our hands on other people. It's also not a part of our culture. A recent study showed that people sitting in a café in Puerto Rico touched each other an average of 189 times per hour. Per hour! The same study in the United States showed we touch each other a measly 2 times per hour.[4]

Donnie showed me firsthand the healing power of touch. It's a way people give and receive love. Sure, it can feel weird, and, yes, you need to make sure it's appropriate, but can we all agree to take a risk when it comes to connecting physically with other humans?

A pat on the back. A squeeze on the shoulder. A hug. A long, long hug. In the early church, people greeted each other with a holy kiss. They were not ashamed of their bodies. They understood we are not just spiritual creatures but also physical ones. We give and receive love through touch.

So wherever you're at in this, take the next step. For you, it might be having the courage to place an affirming hand on someone's shoulder. It might mean to hug a friend. To kiss your son. To put your arm around a hurting friend. To hold the hand of someone going through a loss. To fist-bump someone who is scared.

Jesus could have healed everyone with a word. He had the power to do long-distance miracles, but when the time was right, he touched people. Because sometimes that is the love and healing we need.

A friend told me about the day he was baptized. He was pretty new at the church and didn't know many people. In fact, he knew no one. Because of the choices he'd made, he was pretty much alone in his city.

Then came one of those mushy moments when churches ask everyone to reach across the aisles and hold hands. I know, totally cheesy church thing, right? My friend was in a sparsely filled section of the auditorium, so he figured he'd ignore this part. But a little girl, maybe eight or nine years old, pulled her family all the way down the aisle. She took my friend's hand. And in that moment a strange rush of emotion came over him. A warmth. A belonging. Love. He fought to hold back the tears. Reflecting later, he said, "I think it's because it was the first time I had felt another human's touch in a very long time."

Never ever underestimate the power of a handshake, a pat, a hug. It means you belong. It means you matter. It means you are loved. There are people in your life who don't need your prayer, your words, or even your time. They need your holy, healing touch. The touch of God.

Build up with words.

Donnie's favorite words were "I love you." He was the initiator. The leader. He bravely told you up-front that you were fine and dandy with him. That he was glad you were there, glad you were alive. A treasure. It changed the air of that room, perfuming it with joy.

Why are we so stingy with our words? Why don't we praise people more often? Thank people more often? Compliment their appearance, call out their bravery, and cheerlead their passions?

Maybe they will think we are being manipulative? Brown-nosing the boss? Do we think that lifting up others makes us lower? I don't know. All I know is that it takes about the same amount of energy to say something nice as it does to say something critical.

Our words are like matches. They are cheap but can start fires. These fires can either warm people up or burn them down. They can be campfires for people to gather around or acts of spiritual arson.

Use your words to affirm people. Not just who they are but also who they can become. If you have feelings for people, tell them. Admire them. Gush. Be foolish. Make them feel weird. Toss out the "I love you's" like a drunk millionaire tosses out hundred-dollar bills on the way to his limo. Be rich in love. Be rich in words of affirmation.

This is a habit that grows and draws more and more people.

As you grow fluent in building up others with your words, your campfire will draw more people and give more warmth.

Leave a tangible token of love.

Do you know how to tell if others receive love through giving? They are givers. They are always dropping off gifts and saying "This reminded me of you" or "I just knew you had to have it." Sometimes these are big gift-giving events, like when a friend buys another friend a new set of drums because the old kit was stolen. Most of the time, though, they are smaller experiences, littler things. Tickets to an event. A book. A plate of chocolate chip cookies. A knickknack.

Sometimes the gifts we give aren't traditional gifts at all. There are some people who love to give away stories or beautiful songs or hopeful poems. Every artist is first and foremost a giver—someone who wants to delight others with her or his work. Cooks are perhaps my favorite givers of all.

The point is this: one way to love someone is to give an unexpected, undeserved gift. The more you do it, the better you get at it and the more you put on God's party for others.

LOVING LIKE DONNIE

We are all invited to participate in this love, but sometimes people need handles to grab on to it. You don't have to be comfortable with providing or receiving these love handles to start with; you just have to brave the weirdness until it turns into wonder. God's radical love is calling to you in the off-key voice of someone already enjoying the festivities: "Come away with me. It's not too late for you."

This past Christmas season I received an unexpected text from Jon in Kentucky. His small group was doing their annual

Christmas party once again. He sent me a quick photo of Donnie from the night's celebration. He was standing in the hallway with a huge bearded grin. I smiled as I took in the glory of his Christmas sweater and wondered who would be wrapped up in God's love that night.

YOUR SCARS ARE YOUR TROPHIES

THEY DECLARE YOU FOUGHT HARD TO TELL YOUR STORY OF HOPE

MIKE FOSTER

Six

Change the Mixtape

I want to talk now about mixtapes. They were the 1980s version of a playlist, but instead of living in iTunes, they lived on good old-fashioned plastic cassettes. When a cassette broke, you didn't take it to the Apple Genius bar. You took a number-2 yellow pencil, stuck it in one of the sprockets, and spun it around. *Boom,* you were back in business.

If you've seen the movie *Guardians of the Galaxy,* then you've seen a mixtape in action and know how precious they can be. Star-Lord is willing to risk his life to get back his sweet collection of tunes custom made for him by his mom. Mixtapes were like that. They were personal. They were cherished.

Talking about mixtapes makes me feel really old. I might as well be wearing pleated Dockers and a fanny pack. (No offense to those who still wear pleated Dockers and a fanny pack.)

But I am a child of the 1980s. *Star Wars* and Luke Skywalker. *The Love Boat* with Captain Stubing and his daughter Vicki (whom I had a slight crush on). Love was always happening out on the high seas. I also loved *Fantasy Island* with the white suits and matching shoes and Mr. Roarke with his suave Latin accent. Everything was going to be okay if Mr. Roarke said it was going to be okay. He taught my childhood brain how the world and dreams and fantasies really worked. And let's not forget Magnum driving his red Ferrari and living in a rich guy's house for free. He was the coolest guy in Hawaii and always solved the case.

I also loved my mixtapes.

I would load my favorite songs from my favorite bands all in a row: Culture Club, REO Speedwagon, Bon Jovi. Then I would play that mixtape nonstop in my big gray boom box. I played it so much I wore the tape out. The tape just gave up one day. It got eaten by the player and never played again.

But we have a different kind of mixtape these days. It doesn't play the awesome melodies of REO Speedwagon or Journey. I'm not even talking about iPods, Sirius, or Spotify. No, these mixtapes are invisible, and they play in our heads and hearts. They play up our fears and insecurities. They play a soundtrack of our failures.

They pump out the discouraging tunes of self-hatred with lyrics like . . .

I need to ________ better.
I should be further along than I am.
My life doesn't matter.

Have you heard these songs before? They strip our stories of hope and life. They drown out possibility.

I'm not sure where these tapes come from, but I know a lot about them. Every verse. Every chorus. Every melody. Every bridge back into the chorus. It's all pure evil echoing inside our brains like elevator music.

And have you noticed this about your mixtape? The messages aren't that creative. The lyrics aren't catchy or original. They are like a horrible jingle that gets stuck in your head. They repeat the same thing over and over again. "You stink. You stink. You stink." It's like being stuck on the It's a Small World ride at Disneyland, but the music you keep hearing sings, "You're a loser after all. You're a loo-hoo-serrrr."

How unoriginal. What crappy content. How long do you think we should listen to it?

A couple of months ago I was sitting in my office, and my negative mixtape started to play. It had been a discouraging season. A few triggers here and there. Reasons to doubt myself. Throw in a few pinches of doubt and worry, and I found myself in a low place.

I felt inadequate and lonely.

You're a loser after all. . . .

Our organization was taking on water and sinking. Finances were scary. I took full responsibility.

You're a loser after all. . . .

I felt like an idiot, embarrassed by it all. The picture in my head wasn't working out like it was supposed to.

You're a loser after all. . . .

So you know what I thought? I thought what every leader thinks when the mixtape is playing at full blast. I said to myself, *I should just quit and get a job at Starbucks, because the baristas there look like they are having a lot more fun than I'm having right now.* Good health insurance. Fun atmosphere. Make cappuccino all day. I would just disappear into the world of Howard Schultz and green aprons.

But then I realized I didn't need a new life or a new job. I needed a new soundtrack. I needed to deal with the mixtape in my head.

I started seeing a Christian counselor, and I realized how

messed up and ugly my mixtape was. My self-doubt sounded so normal to me, but it was totally whacked.

My counselor said, "Mike, you write about grace. You preach about grace. You desperately want grace for other people. Isn't it about time you started smoking what you're selling? Maybe it's time for you to get a little grace for yourself."

FEELING THE MUSIC

Let me ask you a question. And be honest. What is your mixtape playing right now? Can you step back and look at your thoughts for just a moment and see what they are doing to you? Can you see the damage being done? Are you tired of listening to the tape?

There's an old adage in moviemaking: "You watch the film but you feel the music." The soundtrack has incredible influence on how we emotionally respond to the events we're seeing on the screen. Try watching a movie with the sound off. Not quite the same.

In the same way, our mental mixtapes provide the music for the things that happen to us. They can make us feel horrible about events that aren't horrible at all or at least aren't as bad as all that. We live our life, but we *feel* the music.

So how can we swap out the gloomy, doubt-filled mixtapes that play in the background of our heads and hearts?

Call baloney on the lyrics.

Just because Jon Bon Jovi sang that he's a cowboy and that he's wanted dead or alive doesn't mean it's true.[1] In fact, Bon Jovi lied to make a great song.

Calling out your own tape as being filled with half-truths, distorted pictures, and outright lies is where you should start. Your self-doubts represent only one version of reality. It's not fact but a point of view, just as a song is only what one artist wants to say. Do the more degrading examples of gangsta rap clearly and truthfully define the value of a woman? Does country music have the sole truth on what a broken heart looks like? Nope, they represent just the songwriters' opinions. And singing a song over and over again doesn't make it true. It just makes it harder to ignore.

Take control of the buttons.

I know, I know. It's nice to think we are powerless victims who have no choice but to wallow in self-hatred. It's convenient since it requires no action on our part. Many of us chose a destructive soundtrack for our lives and actually like the beat and the vibe. It feels familiar. It's all we know. But just like my gray boom box, the music in our head has buttons such as Play, Pause, and Stop. More important, we have a Record button.

If you pushed the red Record button and the Play button on my boom box at the same time, something amazing happened. A new song recorded itself over the old song. So when Madonna stopped being awesome, and I was sick of listening to "Lucky Star," I could smash down the Play and Record buttons and cover it up with the Beastie Boys' *Licensed to Ill.* On the same tape! I could also hit the Eject button and pop in a fresh cassette, but either way you get my point.

We have buttons. We get to choose which buttons we push. When the song wears out or it wears us out, we can change it. It doesn't matter how much we love a song, we can still get tired of it. Trust me, even the best song in the world can start to feel stale.

I always wonder how bands like U2 and the Rolling Stones keep playing the same hits over and over again. The fans demand it. So U2 must play "Where the Streets Have No Name" and the Rolling Stones must play "I Can't Get No Satisfaction." Sure, they might remix it, do an acoustic version, or change up the melody a bit, but they still have to play that song. It must get really old. Just like telling yourself over and over again, "You're stupid. You're hopeless. It will always be this way." It grows tiring.

Some of us have stopped listening to the words on our inner mixtapes, but that hasn't stopped their impact. The music is so much a part of us that we feel the effects even though we don't hear the tune. The words that play are no longer the tape's words but our words.

I start thinking, *I* am *a cowboy on a steel horse* and *I* am *wanted dead or alive.* It's no longer a lyric from the mixtape; it is who I am. And that's when it gets really scary, because we end up in a place far from who God made us to be. We end up completely defined by a lie.

THE SONG THAT GOD SINGS

So think about this for a moment. You and I have our mixtapes. We struggle with the soundtracks in our heads. It's hard not to be affected, especially when life is not going well, but here is something to consider. No matter what your tape says about you, God says something quite different. He says he likes you just the way you are. I know it is sometimes hard to believe that God is proud of you, that he loves you. But this is the song he sings over you. It's the soundtrack of grace.

I once heard of a survey that asked a bunch of Christians what they believed God thought about them. What is the emotion he feels toward Christians? It's a good question. You know what the survey revealed? It was kinda shocking, honestly. The majority of people who responded to the survey basically said, "When God thinks about me, the overwhelming feeling he has is disappointment."

Disappointment. Can you believe that? After all the sermons and songs and devotions and bumper stickers and Bible verses we read about God's love, we still think he is disappointed with us. How horrible! What an indictment on what's going on right now. Because here's the truth: if you think God feels disappointment when he looks at you, then you don't know God very well. It's time to throw out that song and start over.

We need to start listening to the mixtape of grace and eject the Enemy's mixtape of shame. If the voice you hear in your head is one of condemnation, you can be sure it's not the voice of God.

And you know what else I've learned? There is nothing holy, spiritual, or godly about beating yourself up. Beating yourself up is *not* a fruit of the Spirit. Talking bad to yourself is not a spiritual solution. It's a symptom of a spiritual problem that God's love song is meant to fix.

When you find yourself dying under the doleful tunes on your lousy mixtape, feeling like a failure, a nothing on the way to nowhere, hit Pause. Stop listening to yourself, and start talking to yourself. Say, "So what if I'm a hypocrite and feel like a fraud? So what if the Enemy on my mixtape wants to play his tune? Let that accuser sling his lies and accusations. Let him blacklist me and shame me, 'cuz whatever the accuser throws my way is just a tape. A tape I can stop, eject, record over. I want to listen to a different tape. A different song. A rockin' tune that reminds me I am whole, free, and forgiven. I am heaven's poetry. I am God's beloved, and he sings over me."

REIMAGINING YOUR LIFE

Did you ever play make-believe as a kid? Set up tea parties for animals? Construct whole worlds out of blocks or Legos? Establish complex social lives using only dolls and Barbie figures?

I used to love playing good guys versus bad guys. I'd flip my gun (a Nerf gun) out of the holster or run and hide in my fort (the closet). My horse (a tricycle) and I would go on grand adventures through the desert (the backyard), and I'd be breathless on my return to home base (the kitchen) because I had barely made it back alive.

A lot of people think we lose this ability to participate in make-believe as we get older, but research suggests it moves from the outside world of play to the inner world of thoughts and reasoning. Pamela Weintraub calls this inner narration "self-talk" and notes that it greatly affects the way we interact with the world.[2]

Laura Berk, at the University of Southern Illinois, believes that this self-talk we inherit from childhood sets the stage for self-control in adulthood. Our make-believe play teaches children how to distance themselves from reality. The more kids use their imaginations in childhood, the better they are at separating themselves from stressful situations later in life.[3]

As adults, we need to find a space in our brain to separate our emotions from what's happening in our lives. We need to use our imaginations to become temporary bystanders in stressful situations. That way, we can respond to the problem without being dominated by worry or anxiety.

Worry is the problem after the problem. Anxiety is self-talk gone wrong. You are engaging in make-believe every time you face an issue. You may as well spin it to your advantage.

Studies show that worry does not have to be automatic. Self-doubt can be reversed. You just need to learn to use your imagination for good, not bad.

Here's an amazing example. Psychologist Ethan Kross asked eighty-nine men and women to give a speech about why they were the perfect candidates for their dream jobs. Half of the group was directed to use only personal pronouns, such as *I* and *me,* as they prepared. The other half was told to complete their preparation using their actual names.[4]

Basically, this second group had to talk about themselves as if they were somebody else—the way certain athletes talk about themselves in the third person. "I wanted to do what was best for LeBron James, and to do what makes LeBron James happy," said LeBron James.[5] We joke about this, but it works.

Those who used their actual names seemed to have a greater amount of confidence. They even started talking to themselves in the third person, saying things like "You can do it, Ethan" and "You've got this, Suzie."

The people who used their actual names not only performed better on their speeches but also didn't think about it as much once the speech was done. They experienced less depression and felt less shame.

Here is Kross's conclusion:

> When dealing with strong emotions, taking a step back and becoming a detached observer can help.[6]

UNFLIPPING THE I SWITCH

It would appear that all of us have a switch in our brain that makes us lose almost all objectivity and a good deal of common sense about our own situations. It's the word *I.* So short. I mean, it's just a line. In fact, it looks a little like a switch, doesn't it?

Whenever you speak to yourself as an "I," every emotion or dark thought that comes to mind is instantly a part of you. Every fear is real. Every shortcoming is massive. Every flaw glaring.

Like when you have a zit. It may be only a tiny blip on your skin, but the embarrassment you feel makes it seem as if it's your whole face. You think, *Everyone sees this. All I am is one big zit!* Meanwhile, people are passing by and not noticing at all, feeling like big zits themselves.

This is the problem with the I switch. But the cool thing is that we can unflip it just by changing the self-talk we use. The next time you feel like a loser, take your most negative I thought, like *I'm never going be good enough,* and slip your actual name in there:

Julie will never be good enough.

Eric sucks.

Emily is a loser.

Brandon will never find love.

Notice how it starts to sound silly? I mean, who says that? Would you put up with another person telling you that? No way!

Next, write it down. Type it out. Just look at it. Now notice how easily you can change it. Just backspace a few times. Get out the Wite-Out. Type something new.

Julie is trying her best.

Eric made a mistake.

Emily is a decent friend and worker.

Brandon is not defined by whom he's dating.

Still think this sounds too simple? Get ready for more science!

Jason Moser, a neuroscientist and clinical psychologist at Michigan State University, says that when we change what we call ourselves, we can turn off what the brain is thinking about us.

Moser noted, "This is not the way we have tried to calm ourselves down in the past, but the studies show it is not necessary to scold the emotional brain. Language creates a distance that is real."[7]

"Scold the emotional brain." Isn't that what we all do? Constant self-shaming? Not only is it icky and joy destroying, but it doesn't work.

If you want to get better and be better, flip the I switch, get a bit of detachment, and deal with the real problem without becoming an emotional casualty.

L'EGGO MY EGGO

The reason we find it hard to separate emotion from issues has to do with the little, psychologically charged word *ego.*

The ego is the part of us that is always fretting about how we look, how we act, and how we are perceived by others. When our feelings get hurt, it is actually our ego that is hurt. And the way our ego finds comfort is to compare itself to others. It finds significance in being more successful, more beautiful, more religious than others.

In other words, your ego is a voracious black hole of need. It is like Bill Murray's character in the movie *What About Bob?* Always shuffling around and mumbling, "I want, I want, I need, I need."[8] It is painfully dependent on outside sources to feel good about itself.

The ego is not evil. It just needs a proper diet of God's love and affirmation. The problems begin when we step away from that relationship and start trying to fill our ego needs with other things.

In his book *The Freedom of Self-Forgetfulness,* Tim Keller describes the natural state of God-detached egos as "empty, painful, busy and fragile."[9] We either look down our noses at other people or imagine them looking down their noses at us. Both attitudes result from a famished ego starving for God's love. Both are lost in a sea of self.

Keller points out that the apostle Paul dealt with this issue of ego head-on. Paul refused to feed his ego on what others thought. He even refused to care about what he thought. Keller frames

Paul's thoughts like this: "I don't care what you think—but I don't care what *I* think. I have a very low opinion of me—but I have a very low opinion of *my* opinion of me."[10]

Paul didn't give much credence to his mess-ups or successes, only to grace. He didn't fuse his sins or his wins to his identity; he let them roll like water off a duck's back. The only thing that stuck was God's unexplainable love. It was the only food he gave his hungry, hungry ego.

Keller concludes: "True gospel-humility means I stop connecting every experience, every conversation, with myself. In fact, I stop thinking about myself."[11]

God brings the "*ultimate* verdict" of who we are, and that verdict declares us important and valuable.[12] The gospel is the only religion that gives the verdict before the performance. It's not about trying to be good enough. It's about God *already* being good enough. It's about the verdict already being in. The trial is over. The reviews are already in. No need to perform. We've been credited with five stars.

FREEING YOUR LIGHT

Long ago young children in Hawaii were told the parable of the bowl of light.[13]

Each child was said to have a bowl of perfect light. If the children respected and loved their bowls of light, they would grow in strength and health and could swim with sharks, fly with birds, and know and understand all things. If, however, the children got into trouble, with thoughts of fear, worry, doubt, judgment, anger, resentment, envy, or jealousy, they would drop a stone into the bowls of light. And some of the light would go out of the bowl, because light and stone cannot occupy the same space. If a child continued to collect stones in the bowl, the light would eventually go out, and the child would become a stone. And like a stone, the child would no longer grow or be capable of movement.

As soon as the child grew tired of being a stone, however, all that was needed was *kalana,* the Hawaiian word for "forgiveness." It also means release from a wrong. The child would forgive this aspect of himself or herself by turning the bowl upside down and letting the stones fall out. All the light could then shine again and grow even brighter than before.

The parable contained two powerful lessons for the children. One, each and every one of them had a light, a unique identity. And two, it was their responsibility, and theirs alone, to empty the stones so their light could be fully known.

It's time to change the mixtape in our heads. To silence the voices of inner shame and judgment. To start using self-talk to our own advantage. To feed our egos on the unending love of God rather than the fickle opinions of others.

And above all, we must forgive ourselves. Dump out the stones. Wash out our bowls. The world needs our light.

YOU HAVE THE LIFE YOU ARE WILLING TO TOLERATE. IF YOU WANT *more*, PURSUE IT.

MIKE FOSTER

Seven

Accept Your Fifty-One Status

I was in Carmel, California, at a leadership retreat at the James House, a historic home perched on the cliffs overlooking the Pacific Ocean. The setting could not have been more amazing, with bald eagles floating on the wind, butterflies dancing on wildflowers, and white-foamed waves crashing on the jagged rocks below. Seriously, this place is epic. A slice of heaven on earth.

My friend Mark hosted the event. He runs an organization that connects like-minded individuals doing good stuff in the world. Artists, entrepreneurs, nonprofit leaders, and a couple of pastors were in attendance. My friend Dave, a best-selling author, came for that weekend. So did Joshua, who gets paid to take pictures of Sting and Carrie Underwood. My friend Shannon, a human-rights activist, and my mentor, Bill, an entrepreneur in the energy sector, were all there. We talked and talked and laughed and laughed. We had no agenda but to enjoy one another's company.

On the first morning we all gathered at the breakfast table in the kitchen. A fire roared in the fireplace as we sat in creaking chairs at an antique table. We gobbled down eggs and French toast. We sipped coffee and orange juice. It was a true communal experience. So casual. So relaxed.

Then everyone started talking about something that made me feel like an outsider. The topic was a gift package Mark had recently sent to everyone there. It included some African coffee, a couple of books, and other cool knickknacks from some non-profits Mark works with.

My friends Shannon and Bill raved about how awesome the goody bag was and how great the African coffee tasted. They gushed. And gushed. Everyone knew exactly what they were talking about.

Everyone except me.

Ever been in one of those conversations where you wish you could say something or add something, but if you do, you risk exposing the fact that you have no idea what you're talking about? That was me. So I was silent.

Shannon noticed my silence and lobbed a mercy ball, trying to get poor me involved in the conversation game. "Mike," she said, "wasn't that goody bag awesome?"

I looked back at her and said: "Well, it sounds sweet, but I don't have any idea what you all are talking about. I don't think I got the package."

Mark quickly chimed in. "Well, I sent it to you. I know I did. Are you sure you didn't get it?" He seemed almost indignant and combative.

I replied sheepishly. "Nope. I didn't see anything in the mail, Mark. The gifts sound really great, but I'm pretty certain I never received anything from you."

He replied emphatically, "Well, that's weird. I know I sent it to you. I sent it to my top fifty friends and influencers. I know you're on that list, Mike."

(Okay, I need to stop here a second. Sorry to interrupt the story, but can we all agree that it's weird to have a numeric list of friends? And that it's even weirder to rank them? Moving on . . .)

Mark whipped out his laptop, popped open a spreadsheet, and began scrolling down a list. It was filled with names and addresses. I knew a lot of the people on the list. Friends and others I've bumped into over the years. Great folks, every one of them. I never saw who was number one. Maybe Jesus was the first name? We shall never know.

Mark scrolled down, looking for my name, insisting I was on the list. He flipped his laptop around so the others and I could see it and help him find my name. He whispered under his breath, "I know you're here somewhere. I know I sent it to my top fifty. I know I sent it."

At this point everyone at the table was engaged in solving this great mystery. Why didn't Mike get the package? Why has everyone at the table been enjoying goody-bag knickknacks while Mike never got them?

Mark scrolled and scrolled. And then the mystery was solved in one pure, unadulterated, hard-truth moment. Mark was right. He had sent it to the top fifty friends. But there, on line fifty-one of his spreadsheet, was this name: *Mike Foster.*

I was number fifty-one.

Fifty. Stinkin'. One!

I didn't get the package because I didn't make the cut. I wasn't in the top fifty.

At this point everyone looked at one another with awkward, shame-filled glances. They had all made the list. I had not. They were in. Mike was out.

It was like that elementary-school moment when your fifth-grade class lines up and picks teams to play kickball. The teacher chooses a captain for each team, thus giving these lucky ones godlike powers. The captains now have the power to crown you with glorious value by selecting you in their first few picks. The captains also hold the power to reduce your value to zero by picking you last, forever branding you as a kickball reject. It sets up your pattern for life. Your ruler of self-worth. "Whatever happens, don't get picked last." Don't be a leftover.

The real goal of elementary-school athletics had nothing to do with the actual play on the field. It wasn't even about the score of the game or winning. The only thing that mattered, the only real competition was making sure you were not picked last. It was like the Hunger Games only without all the blood and death and Jennifer Lawrence.

"I'll take David."

"All right, then I choose Johnny."

"Hmm, okay, I pick Scott."

"Happy Hunger Games! And may the odds be ever in your favor."

How do I know how this works? Because I was picked last a bunch of times at various sporting events on playgrounds. I have long worn the scarlet number of fifty-one.

And I bet at times you have too, right? You know how it feels. We all know what it's like to be fifty-first. The leftovers. No one cared if we were on the team or where we stood on the field. We were a mild nuisance that made no difference in the competition.

So there we were, a group of professional adults sitting around a breakfast table feeling like we were back in elementary school on kickball day. They had all been picked. I had not.

How do you respond to the not-quite-good-enougher seated with you at the breakfast table? Some stared at their eggs. Others glared at Mark for even having such a list. A few quietly reached for their cooling coffee.

But then, as friends do when they're stuck in a moment they can't get out of, someone started to giggle. And then another. It built into outright laughter, till the whole room was roaring. This was too absurd a moment not to find the humor and insanity of everything it contained. It was absolutely ridiculous. Positively laughable. And so we laughed. All in honor of number fifty-one.

LAUGHING AT THE LISTS

You will encounter a lot of lists in your life. Some are written on spreadsheets, others are written into our culture, and many are written in our hearts.

The VIP and almost VIPs.

The ins and outs.

The welcomed and the left-outs.

The white sheep and the black sheep.

The do-gooders and the not-enoughers.

We all live with the fear of not cutting it. Not getting in. Not belonging or being loved. It's such a devastating thought that we do everything in our power to wiggle and wrangle and sneak our way onto the team. Then work our way to the top.

The *college list* says go to a respected school. Don't get wasted too much, and figure out a way to graduate. If you have that piece of paper, you're in the club and doors open up. Even if that means leveraging your future with a six-figure student loan, get on the list.

The *career list* demands you come in early and stay late. Performance is key, and don't forget you're lucky to be picked. If you're not happy or don't cut it, we have a hundred more waiting in the wings to take your place.

The *sexy list* requires you to give it all you've got to craft a smoking bod. The more heads you turn, the more you're worth. If you can't fit into your skinny clothes or if you're not buffed or curved in the right places, you are off the list. Start looking old, and your days are numbered.

The *popular list* says to get noticed at all costs. If you don't have a platform or a list of followers, you are nobody. No views, no hits, no likes—you are out of luck. Only movers and shakers belong on this list, and you have no influence.

I can go on and on. Whatever group you want to be a part of has a list. There are things you must do, approvals you must gain, or you are out. Lists demand you do what it takes to be included.

But the good news of Jesus is that his grace makes a joke out of every other list designed to give or deny value to human beings. Lists are laughable, just like my being number fifty-one. They don't deserve respect. They deserve a hilarious chuckle.

Paul puts it this way in Galatians 3:28: "There is no longer Jew or Gentile, slave or free, male and female. For you are all one in Christ Jesus." So the only list that matters now is the list of human beings whom Christ loves, and the last time I checked, that's a tiny group of people called *everyone.*

The great tragedy is that the very group meant to laugh at all the lists—the church—seems bent on making more of them. Rather than sharing God's love, we make more lists.

The Traditional Church List

- No sandals allowed.
- Shower and deodorant required.
- Tithe.
- Read the Bible. (And not just the fun parts!)
- Appear to have no sin.
- Tithe.

- Do everything the church says.
- Believe everything the pastor says without question. (Even the cray-cray stuff.)
- Did we mention tithing?

Freer, more "spiritual" Christians have their own lists of what it means to be a real believer.

The Progressive Christian List

- Pick at least one social cause and talk about it all the time.
- Deodorant optional.
- No gas-guzzling, environment-destroying SUVs.
- Mistrust churches, especially big ones.
- Glorify poverty.
- No Dockers.
- Disagree with any and all moral obligations.
- Extra credit for owning an original pair of Toms.

We love our lists. Especially when we are the ones making them. Make the list and you get to pick. But that is not what Jesus was about. It's not what we, as the church, should be about.

One of my favorite Shel Silverstein poems is titled "Fourth Place." It's spunky and funny and perfectly captures the essence of being on the outside and not making the cut. It ends like this:

I came in *fourth* in a beauty contest
And there were just *three* of us in it.[1]

It's funny in a poem but tragic in practice.

The church is not meant to be a place where people constantly get the message that they've come in fourth place when only three were competing. It's not a place where lists keep people from seeing that Jesus has chosen them for his love.

Second chancers see things differently. We stir the pot of hope and burn the lists in the flames of grace. And when we pick teams, we say that everyone who wants to play gets to play. Just get out on the field and have fun. Make sure you get some grass stains on those pants by sliding into home, because if you're going to play, we need you to *really* play. Everyone is the first pick, and everyone will get the trophy. The best part of all: no one is keeping score. Seriously, no scorecard here. Just enjoy yourself.

THE LONG SEARCH FOR RIGHT HERE

The Bible says that God is in us. Around us. Before us and behind us. Working for us. Working through us. He is "in here." And we are in him. We are standing in the middle of the party he's throwing. The party master welcomes us to new life where God is for us!

And that means he's also in others. Our neighbors. The school bus drivers and grocery clerks. The guy popping his gum and the girl rolling her eyes. They all contain God too. It seems we never have to look far to find him.

When we search for God in far-off places, we say it's a noble pursuit, and yet the only real pursuer is the Hound of Heaven. You cannot even chase him until he is first chasing you. God is not a prize you earn with spiritual effort. You are his prize! Seriously, in incomprehensible mercy, the God who needs nothing considers your broken, prodigal little life his pearl of great price.

God is with you. Always. He is in you. In every moment. That's the deal he came to make. But the other part of that deal is that we must lose the lists and embrace love instead.

There is work to be done—the work of loving one another.

Every single person you know, come across, fight with, disagree with, laugh with, or love is an opportunity to learn something about God. Get to know the beauty-pageant fourth placers. Be patient with other languages. Show compassion to different religions. You don't have to search for God; you just need to open your eyes and see him in your neighbor.

God is here right now. You don't have to look far. You just have to look out.

BUILDING BUDDY BENCHES

Second-grader Christian Bucks probably knows a few things about lists and fourth placers and fifty-ones. He knows enough to do something about it. He was aware that some of his classmates felt lonely during recess. Maybe Christian recognized it because he's been lonely too. I guess we all have, right?

But Christian decided to make a place for friendship and support. A place where kids could sit when they felt left out. He pitched the idea to Principal Matthew Miller. Then he presented the concept to his classmates. He said, "What if we had this place on the playground where we could be friends to people who needed friends? If someone was sitting on the bench, then another student could come over and ask if they wanted to play. If maybe they just needed to talk about their feelings, we could sit on the bench and talk with them." The idea was a hit.

Principal Miller let Christian pick the colors and the style of the new friendship bench. Christian also was the first person to sit on the bench. God must have smiled and angels applauded as Roundtown Elementary School caught on to the big idea. No one needs to be alone. No one gets left out anymore.[2]

Our mandate as second chancers and hopesters is to live by this motto: No one alone. We defend the defenseless. Love the loveless. Welcome the outsider. God is in each and every one. He isn't up there. He is right here.

Christian said, "We show we care about others when we ask others to play."[3] And perhaps that's the easiest thing we could ever do for people. Just ask them to play with us. To party with us. When we rally around the lonely and the left out, we shift the shape of the universe. The lists fade away. The contests don't matter anymore. Just come sit on the bench with us.

YOU HAVE NO
loyalty
TO YOUR PAST.
YOU'RE NOT REQUIRED
TO *carry*
IT INTO
today.

MIKE FOSTER

Eight

De-Bacon Your Heart

Bacon is in. It's the cat's meow of breakfast meats—a four-billion-dollar industry in the United States alone. More than 65 percent of Americans would gladly have bacon be named the national food.[1] We devour chocolate-covered bacon, bacon ice cream, brioche bread pudding smothered in bacon sauce . . . and the list goes on.

We indulge in bacon eating with abandon. Arun Gupta from the *Indypendent* noted, "Wendy's 'Baconator,' six strips of bacon mounded atop a half-pound cheeseburger, . . . sold 25 million in its first eight weeks."[2] Comedian Jon Stewart quipped that "baconnaise" is a product "for people who want to get heart disease but [are] too lazy to actually make bacon."[3]

The average American consumes eighteen pounds of bacon each year. When astronaut Buzz Aldrin landed on the moon, his first meal included bacon. But it's not just Americans and astronauts in space who love bacon. A 2010 survey of Canadians found that 43 percent would choose to eat bacon rather than have sex.[4] Eh?

And yet we can't avoid this one huge fact: bacon is bad for us.

Why do we love our bacon so much? We know it's loaded with calories and salt and fat that clog arteries and make us pudgy. Sarah Hepola from Salon.com suggests eating bacon is an act of rebellion: "Loving bacon is like shoving a middle finger in the face of all that is healthy and holy."[5]

For his book *The End of Overeating,* David Kessler interviewed a professor of psychiatry about how combinations of fat and sugar intensify the impact on our brains. Turns out, these two elements operate in a similar manner to cocaine, and when we consume our Baconator sandwich, we are self-administering "stimulating and sedating effects" much like those of a "speedball," an often-deadly combination of cocaine and heroin.[6]

Eating bacon is bad for our health, but we can't stop. The worst part of us craves it.

And judging others is a lot like bacon. It's savory and delectable and clogs your heart.

Both eating bacon and judging others are powerful and addictive. Both have a cultural and personal impact.

Judgmentalism is not good for us, but we gobble it up anyway. It satisfies us for a moment, just like a sugar-and-salt speedball or four strips of sizzling bacon. It fulfills a purpose.

LABELS LIE

I've done a lot of judging in my life, and I know you have too. So we can't pretend there isn't something satisfying or savory about pointing a few fingers and judging a few of our favorite targets. There must be some benefit to it, don't you think? The most obvious is that if I can cut you down a few notches, I soothe my own insecurities. When I find something dirtier than I am, I don't feel as dirty.

It's a formula that works pretty well if you think about. I pick the topic for comparison. I set the standards. I find those who don't meet the standards. I win.

Even the gospel can mistakenly be defined by judgment. Philosopher Alan Watts put it this way: "Religions are divisive and quarrelsome. They are a form of one-upmanship because they depend upon separating the 'saved' from the 'damned,' the true believers from the heretics, the in-group from the out-group. Even religious liberals play the game of 'we're-more-tolerant-than-you.'"[7]

We have so many easy targets in our society, mostly made up of people we do not personally know. Pointing a finger at stereotypes and villainized people groups is a surefire win. Just decide how much you need to feel good, and start the competition.

Single moms at Wal-Mart with out-of-control kids.

McDonald's employees who ride the bus and need free health care.

Conservative Baptists who love the Bible and George Bush.

Girls who sleep around or grown men who still live with their moms.

The homeless, the jobless, and the food stampers.

Mexican border crossers, gay people, and addicts in rehab for the fourth time.

Old lady drivers and people who still pay with checks.

Clamshell flip-phone owners with obnoxious ringtones.

Judgment ensures we pick the most marginalized, the people least able to fight back. But I don't want a trophy from a competition that's been totally rigged, and neither do you. Are you going to flaunt a gold medal that you gave yourself for being awesome, knowing you set up the rules and never actually competed? That's what casting judgment on another person is—a hollow, cowardly victory.

Certainly, my being better than you makes me feel better for a moment. It's electric and euphoric to feel superior to another. It puts my own morality on a pedestal and allows me to shake my head and wag my finger and say, "Thank God I'm not like them." Judgment happens in a moment. In a thought. And it feels so good.

A quick bacon hit. Yummy. Until you start seeing what it's doing to your soul.

And let us not ignore the reason we play the judgment game. We do it to mask our own self-judgment. The way you judge others shows me how you judge yourself.

I've seen it over and over again. The most vengeful, hateful people are always filled with rage and hatred toward themselves. Jesus spoke of this in Luke 6:45 when he said, "A good man brings good things out of the good stored up in his heart, and an evil man brings evil things out of the evil stored up in his heart. For the mouth speaks what the heart is full of" (NIV).

A judged heart judges others. A condemned heart condemns others.

The opposite is also true. A freed heart frees others. A forgiven heart forgives others.

Another reason we judge others is that, as human beings, we want to understand the world. It's crazy out there, with all types of people populating it. God created us to be context-making machines, so our brains are always looking for ways to understand the world and fit pieces together. A label helps us quickly assess what something is. It helps us "get" people and define who they are. Labeling is a shortcut.

Psychologist Solomon Asch studied how we create biases, judgments, and labels based on limited information about unfamiliar people. As a researcher, he found that most of our labels and biases are automatic. We see a certain behavior in a person, and we make an automatic conclusion. In this automatism we tend to see people as favorable who demonstrate favorable traits and vice versa. If you demonstrate unfavorable traits, well, then you're an unfavorable character.[8]

For example, when we think of a drug addict, we may think of a skinny, unemployed man lying in a ditch somewhere. Unfortunately, this is a skewed view of an addict. Or if I say the word *Baptist,* your brain jumps to a particular and automatic stereotype. We see the label and not the person. It's far easier to judge a simple label than a nuanced human being.

Our mood impacts our biases toward people. If we're in a good mood, we tend to think better of people. If we're in a bad mood, we tend to think worse of people. The worse we feel, the worse people are. And the more "judgy" we become.

But as second chancers, we need to become aware of what our brains are up to. We must resist labels. We should become wary of moral pedestals. We ought to readily admit that we get it wrong a lot of the time.

I get trapped in this kind of label making all the time. My brain starts to razzle-dazzle me with its quick moves and assessments of people. Probably one of my worst bonehead judgments was when I met Jennifer, who later became my wife.

THAT TIME I ALMOST DIDN'T MEET MY WIFE BECAUSE I WAS A JUDGMENTAL JERKFACE

It was a Wednesday night at church. She walked in with Jake, the renowned Don Juan of the group. He had a new girl on his arm almost every week. This particular week he strutted around with a blonde. Jennifer didn't realize she was Jake's catch of the week, but I did.

"Hey, Mike! C'mon on over and meet Jennifer," Jake said from the church foyer.

"Um, all right," I said.

I was polite but standoffish to her, not interested in being warm and hospitable. I just wanted to punch the card for my Christian welcoming duties and get out of there. My brilliant assessment was that Jennifer was a blond floozy and I probably wouldn't see her again. Just the arm candy of the week for Mr. Juan. (Notice all the labels.)

Little did I know Jennifer had just accepted Jesus at a Newsboys concert the weekend before. Yes, I know. Totally crazy, right? At a Newsboys concert? Yep! And don't judge.

Jake was the only person she knew who was into the whole Christian thing. She wanted to start going to church and to get to know God, and Jake had been more than willing to oblige. He had the spiritual gift of womanizing and evangelizing.

In that church foyer I quickly labeled my future wife as a blond floozy. Man, did I get that one wrong. Twenty years of marriage and two kids later, Jennifer is my angel and the most wonderful woman I know. My bacon-loving, label-making brain nearly got me into a lot of trouble on that one.

We also get it wrong with groups of people. I recently watched a YouTube video in which homeless people in Orlando share one fact about themselves that other people wouldn't know just by walking past them. Using Sharpies, they wrote these facts on pieces of cardboard and held them up for the camera.[9]

A fifty-year-old homeless man wearing a safari hat holds a sign that says "I've built robots."

A young mother, wearing baggy black sweats and a blue T-shirt, holds up a sign: "Epileptic seizures for 10 yrs . . . And still fighting!" She stands next to her brown dog and a baby stroller.

A middle-aged woman holds a sign that says "I was a personal trainer believe it or not."

Sign after sign and story after story roll by in the video.

"I am homeless, and I DO have a job."

"I went to modeling school."

"I was on the Buffalo Bills practice squad from 1998–2000."

We jump to conclusions so quickly. If we never ask or engage with people, how can we know the truth about them? This is why we must reserve judgment based on prefab labels and lazy categorization. You don't know others' stories until they share them and you listen without judgment.

LOVE IS STRONGER THAN HATE

Love is way stronger than hate. Acceptance is way more transformational than shame.

You want to change the world around you? Stop demanding what you are owed, and start giving others what they need. Stop clinging to your rights and petty offenses and start seeing others as priceless in the eyes of God.

Hate sees itself as victorious over opposition. Love tries to bring together people who would otherwise be pushed apart. It doesn't demand its own way.

Hate says, "If you don't agree with me, you are my enemy." Love says, "We don't have to agree with each other to love each other." My friend Bob Goff tweeted, "The way we treat people we disagree with the most is a report card on what we've learned about love."[10] Love presses for mutual understanding. It rejoices when the truth wins out.

You and I choose the way of love or the way of hate with every reaction. With every offense. One way gives you immediate feel-good emotions as you transfer that pain onto others, but you also fuel the conflict for another day. The other way, the love way, the path to enemy-free living, absorbs the pain, transforms the pain, and responds with hate-crushing goodness.

Author and monk Thomas Merton said, "Our job is to love others without stopping to inquire whether or not they are worthy. That is not our business. What we are asked to do is to love and this love itself will render both ourselves and our neighbors worthy."[11]

One path keeps your world the way it is. The other transforms it into God's vision for your life. Being a second chancer means granting others the same grace you have received. A second chancer gives other people the space to become second chancers too.

OVERTHROW JUDGMENT, LIBERATE LOVE

One of the lessons I am learning about God and how he shapes my heart is that God does his shaping through the people I love. Through the lives of the other beloved. It's clear to me that when compassion and kindness are brought into my life, it's the hand of God at play. He is moving on my behalf. He is loving me through others.

I know many people have amazing experiences where they feel the love of God firsthand in their hearts. They go off alone and feel his presence, approval, and acceptance in a special and direct way. Maybe you've had one of those moments. I hope you have. I hope everyone does.

Still, I like to think that God's love is always on, is constant. It's not there only when we feel it and think about it or have a really spiritual moment. It's always residing in us. His love, acceptance, and delight in us are ever present. And the key to experiencing even more of this love is to give it away. To let it flow out so we can be filled even more.

I guess God could just rain his love on us. He could set up a direct flow into each and every person's heart. But that's not how he set up the love exchange. We are not just reservoirs of his love and grace. We are channels. We are rivers meant to flow.

You can see the brilliance of this strategy. The more we love others, the more his love spreads out into the world. Maybe that's why Jesus's bottom line on living a powerful life came down to a two-pronged commandment: love God and love others (Matthew 22:34–40). It wasn't just a commandment; it was a description of how life works. The more we love others, the more we experience the love of God.

This is also a clever way to dismantle the beautiful lies of judgment and labels. God has appointed the outsider, the misfit, the other as the primary mechanism for expanding the love inside our hearts. Loving the other is how we get more of him. More life. More of all we are meant for.

God is in the expansion business. He grows our hearts to make more room for love. He upgrades and jumbo-sizes everything that has to do with love. And that love expands our lives.

And that's the real tragedy of a judgmental spirit. It cuts us off from the love and life we are meant to share. Love hosts prodigal parties. Judgment shuts them down.

I AM FAR MORE OFFENSIVE

Think about this for a moment: Jesus was the most right, righteous, and pure person who ever lived. Compared to him, we are all hopelessly wrong and crazy sinful. He must have disagreed with about every insight and inclination of the human hearts he was sent to save. But did he spend his time tsking and sighing and getting fed up? Did he back away and separate himself from people who were less holy than he? Did he unfriend people who couldn't help but say offensive, ridiculous things?

No. Jesus came to embrace the other, the outcast, the notorious losers of the world. I guarantee that whatever offense you have to hate or justification you have to judge, Jesus had infinitely more reason for offense and justification to send away the people he encountered. But that's not what he came to do. He came to restore people, not condemn them. He came to befriend the other and love him, not cast him aside.

Thank God. I am far more offensive to God than anyone could ever be to me. Yet he embraces me. He makes room in his heart for me. And I am grateful for that, and you should be too.

But what about those people Jesus wasn't so friendly with? You know, the Pharisees and those religious-rules dictators? Jesus rarely had time for the legalists and the hyperreligious. And it wasn't because he did not love them. It was that he refused to participate in the system they supported. A system of oppression and judgment and religious self-sufficiency.

He had no space in his appointment book for them because they had no need for what he offered.

Being second chancers, we need to follow his example to love. We need to follow his commands. Otherwise, why on earth do we call ourselves his followers at all?

I live out my second-chance life by this truth: *My mission in life is not to be right but to be loving.* This is the choice I make every day as best I can. The facts aren't as precious to me anymore. I bumped so hard into God's grace that it freed me from living a life of black and white.

One of my favorite scenes in the Disney movie *Inside Out* is when Joy, Sadness, and their tour guide, Bing Bong, are riding on "the train of thought." In their rush to get back to headquarters, Joy accidentally spills a box of facts and opinions puzzle pieces. She frantically attempts to get the scattered pieces back into the right places.

She says, "Ugh! These facts and opinions got all mixed up. They look so similar."

Bing Bong reassures her, "Eh. Don't worry. Happens all the time."[12]

Caitlyn Jenner, gay activists, Confederate flag wavers, illegal immigrants, welfare moochers, and religious nut jobs are all meant to extract greater love from my grace-soaked soul. Plain and simple. Sharing my opinion is optional. Sharing my love is not.

TIPS FOR CREATING A JUDGMENT-FREE ZONE

God is on the move in all kinds of situations, so as second chancers we must embrace them. Let me offer some simple ideas for creating a judgment-free zone.

Slow down.

I can't tell you how much my life has benefited from going slow with people. My biggest relational misfires have come from jumping too quickly in my assessments of others. I am grateful that in taking time with them I could dismantle my biases, labels, and misconceptions of lovely people. Listening to their stories, hearing their dreams, knowing their hearts, not just their actions, will help us see people as God sees them.

Assume the best of people and let them prove you wrong.

I would love for you to try this: assume that everyone is trying to do good. Why? Because most people are not trying to hurt you. I truly believe that. And if they are trying to hurt you, it's because they don't know better. People often make decisions out of fear and anger. If we would work to uncover people's real intentions when they say and do things, our relationships would grow so much stronger. Until then, let love be your guide.

Replace judgment with love.

Boy, Mike, that sure sounds simplistic.

Well, that's what's so beautiful about the concept. It's so crazy simple that you can do it. You can start today!

I believe that just as we are all natural-born context-making machines (trying to figure out who is good and who is bad), we are also natural-born love machines. Your capacity to love is equal to your capacity to hate. If there is room enough in your heart to condemn, then there is just as much room for compassion. They are two sides of the same coin. You just need to flip it.

LUNCH WITH OUR ENEMIES

The success or failure of replacing judgment with love will depend on what you cultivate in your relationships. If you choose to be silent, not engage, and ask no questions, then you will have a hard time seeing yourself in the other. But if you slow down, assume the best, and replace snap judgments with snap "lovements," you will start to see your heart grow. The love of God will start to flow to you and through you. Your whole world will begin to expand.

A few years ago I was invited to a lunch with a friend who years earlier had hurt me deeply. Our relationship went horribly wrong. I won't go into all the gory details, but it was one of the biggest betrayals of my life. It caught me completely off guard. I was furious, because he had flipped my whole world upside down. I lost a lot in the debacle—financially, relationally, emotionally. But I also lost a friend, and an enemy was set up in my heart.

Some mutual friends thought it might be a good idea for me and my enemy to reconnect. They knew the details and what a mess it had been for both of us. They invited me to a small lunch to talk. My ex-friend would be there. My first reaction was "Are you kidding? I ain't going if he's there!"

In that moment I forgot I was a second chancer. That I am a follower of the God who expands hearts. That facts and opinions sometimes get mixed up.

So I went to the lunch. I didn't really want to, but I went with an open heart to listen and not fight over facts.

The lunch wasn't easy, but it was necessary. I talked. He talked. I shared openly and honestly. I listened to him. He listened to me. We did not fully accept the other's version of the facts. But that wasn't the point, was it? It was about expanding love and laying off the bacon. 'Cuz that stuff will kill you.

I'M NOT AFRAID OF MY MISTAKES.
I'M AFRAID OF MY EXCUSES.

MIKE FOSTER

Nine

Leave the Garden of Shame

If you're like me, you've probably had a few jobs in your life. I cut lawns during the summer. I washed tiny plastic pots with a toothbrush for a penny each. I had a pool-cleaning business in my twenties. I worked at the Disneyland Hotel bell desk and even drove those iconic brown UPS trucks during the Christmas rush. These jobs all had their ups and downs, but the job I'd most like to forget is my time at Pasta Palace.

Hard to admit, but true. I was part of a system that served mediocre Italian food to myriad unsuspecting families.

I started at the lowest of the low positions: door opener. I would stand by the door and say, "Welcome to the Pasta Palace" six hours a day. That was my gig.

I felt I could do more. I believed I was more than a door opener. The problem was, my grumpy boss didn't think so. Bart was an unhappy middle-aged man who probably dreamed of running a P.F. Chang's or perhaps a Ruth's Chris Steak House, but he was stuck overseeing chefs and their soggy fettuccini, druggie dishwashers, and food servers who complained daily about their shift schedules. His misery soaked the entire place with apathy and despair.

I believed if he would just promote me to waiter, I could really bring new life to this place. I would dazzle customers with my charm and all-you-can-eat salads. I would hustle to get those stuffed mushrooms and calamari appetizers out to the table lickety-split. I would learn everyone's name and bring so much pizzazz to the daily special that my customers would actually believe it *was* something special.

Plus, I would make more money.

Finally, Bart invited me into his office. He said, "Mike, you've been doing a solid job as the greeter."

"Thanks," I said, waiting with eager expectation. This was my moment! I could sense something big was coming.

"I've decided to promote you to a new position," he said, pulling a drag off his morning cigarette.

"Wow! Thanks so much," I responded. A thousand things rushed through my brain at that moment. My dream was coming true. I would wear the official green Pasta Palace apron. With my own engraved nametag. I envisioned the corporate gods honoring me with the Waiter of the Year Award and having me teach the other employees how not to complain about their shifts and how doing drugs and cleaning dishes was a recipe for disaster.

And of course the tips. Oh, the money I would make!

"Mike, now, you won't make any more money at your new position." Bart took another drag from his cigarette.

I chuckled and said, "But, Bart, I *will* be making more money. You just wait and see. I'm going to be an incredible waiter. And when you are an incredible waiter, you make incredible tips, right?"

He grew grumpier. "Mike, you're not going to be a waiter. I'm not even hiring waiters right now, and you're just a door opener. You gotta work your way up to that kind of thing."

"Oh, really?" I replied. The winds of change blew right out of the office, and now only the stink of garlic and cigarette smoke remained. I was crushed. And it was about to get worse.

"No, Mike, you're going to be the new mascot in the front lobby."

"Mascot?" I sheepishly responded. "I didn't know Pasta Palace had a mascot."

"We do now. And guess what, Mike. You're it! Ha, ha, ha!" Bart's lungs crackled and wheezed as he tried to catch his breath.

The costume was ridiculous. It made me look like Chef Boyardee. White pants, white top, red scarf, and a big white floppy chef's hat. My job was to stand by an oven and make tiny pizzas in the main lobby as the guests looked on. Honestly, it was a step down from my door opener position.

There is only one word to describe the emotion I felt as I donned my uniform each day: *shame.*

There is no other feeling quite like shame. It's heavier than humiliation. More sickly than mere embarrassment. More deadly than degradation. And even though one happy day I got to turn in my ridiculous costume and bid farewell to the palace, shame had a way of sticking with me. It's everywhere, really. It got its start in a garden a long time ago.

THE FIRST COVER-UP

Shame showed up very early in the human story. All the way back at the beginning with Adam and Eve. Remember what happened when they ate the forbidden fruit? The first thing they did was grab a few leaves as clothes to hide from each other because they felt—what? Shame. Then they hid from God because they felt—

what? Shame. Then they bickered and blamed and passed the buck for their choices. Why? Shame again.

Bite. Hide. Bicker. Blame. That's the pattern. Sound familiar?

Shame unleashed itself on the world long ago and has been working its dark art ever since. Its most powerful aspect is how undetectable it can be. Shame is so common, so subtle, many times we don't even notice it.

I feel it's time to rip off shame's mask. Let's point a finger at shame and describe it in detail. Lewis Smedes wrote an incredible book on the subject titled *Shame and Grace.* Here's his description:

1. Shame is the persistent feeling that you are not acceptable.
2. Shame is the belief you are less than a good person.
3. Shame is a vague, undefined heaviness that presses on your spirit.
4. Shame is a primal feeling that discolors all other feelings.
5. Shame is the voice repetitively telling you that you don't measure up, so do more.[1]

In other words, shame is what makes you want to cover up. To hide from God. To hide from others.

It touches every human life, including yours.

People often use the words *guilt* and *shame* as though they are the same, but they are different.

Guilt says, "I did something bad." It's the discomfort we feel for violating our own values. Shame says, "I am bad." It's an intense belief that we are flawed and unworthy of love.

Guilt says, "I can do better." It challenges us to grow into what God calls us to be. Shame says, "I am irreversibly broken." It defeats us before we begin.

Guilt says, "I confess." It admits its wrongs and moves on.

Shame says, "I'm fine." It hides behind a wall of false confidence and compensation.

Guilt says, "I'll be forgiven." Shame says, "I'll be rejected."

Guilt can be dealt with through wise counsel, but shame must be healed through love.

HOW WE DEAL WITH OUR NOT-ENOUGHNESS

Do you remember the character Stuart Smalley from *Saturday Night Live*? He wore a powder-blue sweater, sat in a big, soft chair, and stared at himself in the mirror, chanting, "I'm good enough, I'm smart enough, and, doggone it, people like me."

People come up with all kinds of ways to deal with the shame they feel. In fact, I'd say that most of our misery and relational dysfunction comes from our lame efforts to cover up our not-enoughness. Here are three things you probably do to cover your shame:

Strategy 1: Give yourself a trophy.

This strategy says that if you tell yourself often enough, "I'm awesome," you will heal your broken heart. A lot of well-meaning people will tell you, "You just gotta pump yourself up! Think good thoughts. Turn that frown upside down!" But the problem with shame is that it has a hold on your heart, not your head. You can give yourself a thousand trophies a day, and it won't override the feeling that you are a loser. No amount of earning, achievement, or personal effort can fill the gap that shame creates. Trust me, I've tried.

Strategy 2: Give yourself an excuse.

People will also try to minimize their feelings of shame by shifting the blame. Rather than deal with the emotions of unworthiness, they lash out at others. They play the victim. Blame is an effective way for people to discharge their pain. But playing the victim doesn't heal the shame. It just keeps you trapped in a cycle of powerlessness. Giving yourself an excuse will never give you freedom.

Strategy 3: Give yourself an escape.

Heavy, crippling feelings of shame are supposedly solved by avoidance. People escape into sex, substance abuse, social media, pills, video games, food, Netflix binges, and even shopping. Rather than face the shame, we numb ourselves with outside stimuli—quick hits of pleasure to distract our hearts from the nagging sense that we are deeply broken.

The problem with these three strategies is in the word *self.* Shame does not have a self-cure. It only has an "others cure." Help has to come from the outside. Elizabeth Gilbert said it really well: "To be fully seen by somebody, then, and to be loved anyhow—this is a human offering that can border on the miraculous."[2]

That's how we heal shame. Not by covering up, but by opening up and radically accepting one another. We need to remind one another of our core human value and see people not just for who they are in God's eyes but for what they can become.

I've seen it time and time again. When you offer others a safe place to confess their worst secrets, their most horrible sins, their deepest insecurities and most paralyzing weaknesses, and then you smile, put your arm around them, and tell them you love them, the healing and freedom in that moment is powerful and long lasting. It's lifesaving. Seriously. That term is thrown around a lot. I'm not using *lifesaving* cheaply.

This is what I call the rule of radical acceptance, and it's so simple, so scary simple, that anyone can do it. The effects have been profound in my life and the lives I have had the privilege to help. Unconditional love breaks the spell of shame like nothing else can. In fact, it's the only thing that can. I'm pretty sure God designed it that way. Grace is just an idea until you see it in another person's face. Then it becomes power. A power we can all tap.

But so often we go the other direction. Rather than be shame breakers who celebrate the God-given value of every human being, we become shame makers. We tear others down and pile on. We even make it a pastime.

SHAME SLINGING

I recently came across a funny website where people confessed to the fattest things they have ever done. It's a collection of honest moments of gorging and then hiding in shame.

One woman posted this: "I ate half of a cake once when I should have only one piece. I was horrified and didn't want anyone to know, so I finished the cake, baked a whole new one, forced myself to eat the one allowed piece."[3]

One man shared this: "I once ate almost an entire bucket of those cheese balls then I sat there in my orange shame reflecting on the choices I've made." Someone consoled him by responding, "To keep my fingers from getting orange and gross, I've actually eaten cheese balls/popcorn/Cheetos with a shame spoon."[4]

Have you heard of dog shaming? A little blog popped up where people post pictures of their dogs after moments of bad behavior. The owners put handwritten signs inscribed with the offenses near the guilty canines and then post the pics for all to see.[5]

It began with a guilty-looking dog named Beau posing by a pair of torn-up boxers and a sign that read "I am an underwear eating jerk!"

A wild-looking husky has a sign saying "It's 2 a.m. Let me sing you the song of my people!"

A brown Lab's sign says "I ate a whole tub of Vaseline so I have to wear *these* to prevent greasy butt prints everywhere." He's wearing pink underpants.

Shaming is funny when you direct it at dogs in a fun-loving manner, but the shaming fad is catching on. Now people use their cameras and connectivity to bring an avalanche of web hate and e-scorn on unsuspecting people.

If you are frustrated by people's inconsiderate behavior on an airplane, you can vent at www.passengershaming.com, where others amplify your scorn. Or if you don't like a particular megachurch pastor or big-game hunting or a certain restaurant's policies, you can now throw all your hate and bilge on people you don't know without ever leaving your Facebook feed. Heck, you don't even have to understand the issue; you can just get mad and start slinging! It's fun. It's free. It helps us drain our reservoirs of outrage with a few clicks.

You can take whatever little thing that bothers you, add "shaming" to the end, and it becomes a valid social issue. You can even blog about it! Here are some real examples of nonsense shaming from just one year: snack shaming, attendance shaming, salad shaming, Instagram-filter shaming, selfie shaming, pop music shaming, tattoo shaming, and fit shaming.[6]

Jon Ronson, author of *So You've Been Publicly Shamed,* noted this in his June 2015 TED talk: "You know, when we watch courtroom dramas, we tend to identify with the kindhearted defense attorney, but give us the power, and we become like hanging judges."[7]

The crazy thing about this shaming movement is that it's the attacker's own shame that causes the rage. You attack me for being fat? I shame you for being shallow and vain. You try to make me feel bad for breastfeeding in public? I shame you for being against motherhood and nature. You say I'm stupid for supporting this candidate or issue? You should be ashamed for what you support! You are evil! You are destroying the country!

Rather than scream louder or unfriend half the people in our newsfeed, let's back up a minute and cool our easily offended jets. If people say they do not like your taste in music, that is not shaming; that is a preference. If someone posts #nofilter on an Instagram photo, he or she is not judging you for using that super-cool washed-out effect you love to use. It's not about you at all. Tattoos (and I know this is a controversial topic for some) are a choice. So if you get an ugly or stupid one, I am going to think it's ugly or stupid. It's my point of view, not condemnation. For the sake of fairness, I expect you to do the same thing if you ever see the lotus flower on my lower back.

There are moments in life when someone else is going to make you feel bad about something, but that doesn't necessarily mean you've been shamed. Here are some good questions to ask yourself when you feel offended:

- Is this comment part of a larger systemic oppression to reduce human dignity?
- Does this opinion threaten my livelihood or damage my public reputation?
- Are my physical and mental health affected?

If you answer no to all these questions, you are not being shamed. You just happen to have an opinion about something that's unpopular, maybe even stupid. We all have lots of them.

The reason we get so upset at people who disagree or hold different values is that we all are subconsciously aware of our brokenness. When someone points out a difference, we see it as a deficiency. We think our weaknesses and hurts are liabilities to be covered up and protected, hidden from the world. But what I have learned over the years is that broken things can make broken things beautiful again.

We don't need to hide our flaws. We need to own them. We need to ditch perfectionism and own our imperfectionism.

HOW TO BE AN IMPERFECTIONIST

Have you seen the service where, for a small fee, photo editors will retouch and enhance your child's photo so it's pageant worthy? These services break my heart. I am not judging those who provide these services. I'm just fed up with glamorizing perfection. This pursuit of flawlessness erodes our souls.

We're drowning in a sea of marketing messages that sell us products, services, and ideas by making us feel dissatisfied, discontented, or depressed about who we are and what we have.

"This will make you look better" really means "You don't look so good."

"This will make you smarter" is really "You don't know nearly enough."

"This will make you richer" is actually "You're not seriously going to make do with just that pittance, are you?"

The message is always the same: We will touch up your life to make it pageant worthy 'cuz right now you ain't looking so hot.

We seek perfection in our homes, our relationships, our appearances, and, yes, even our families. Instead of enjoying them, we fixate on making them better without knowing what better even is. The result of all this perfectness is not a better life but a life that drives us to escape. Perfectionism only leads to making things less perfect.

The root of the word for *shame* in Greek means "to disfigure." Shame warps the way people look at themselves. We start to think of ourselves as bad glamour shots that need to be touched up rather than people wonderfully made to bear God's image. We live in the terrifying gap between the misshapen thing we see in the mirror and the perfection we feel is demanded.

Perfection may be necessary when it comes to building an airplane or sending a spacecraft to Mars but not when it comes to people's bodies, especially our children's. And not when it comes to our behavior either, because the simple truth is this: perfection is impossible. It's not attainable. You will never, ever be perfect.

You will be a jerk. You will let others down. You will make lousy decisions. You will hurt others. You will mess up your children. You will have moral failures. You will have horrible memories. You will be rejected. You will be heartbroken. Imperfection is a part of this life, and anyone who tells you otherwise is an imperfect liar!

So if we're going to make life into God's party, we have to ditch this damaging desire to be flawless. We need to get comfortable with our not-so-good sides, our balance of darkness and light. We need to become imperfectionists.

As a second chancer, I believe the disfigurement that takes place with shame is a disfigurement of the plan God desires for our lives. The greatest gift you can give the world is being the person God uniquely created you to be. Let me say that again, because it's something that gets lost in the sauce all day, every day. *The greatest gift you can give the world is to be the person God uniquely created you to be.* That's it. That's the win. Drop the mic and go to Disneyland.

Maybe it is time to start a campaign to help Instagram add a filter called "real" or create a Photoshop setting that increases exposure on inner beauty. While we're at it, let's add a section on LinkedIn where people can post the past work experiences that didn't go so hot.

While these ideas may never happen, we can take action in

the small, everyday choices we make: choices about the products we buy, the ideals we obsess about, and the values we lend our time and energy to.

PERFECTIONISM IS ABOUT AVOIDING SHAME

It's important to remember you aren't a machine or a project or a problem. And neither are other people. You don't need to become someone you are not, and you don't need to be perfect in order to grow. Our imperfections are what make us human, and they help us relate to each other. Or as songwriter Leonard Cohen noted, "That's how the light gets in."[8] It's also the cracks that let the light out. So let's ditch shame and start to shine. Show off your flaws. Share all that you are.

At its core, perfectionism is about avoiding shame. Rather than numb your inadequacy with drugs or escapism, you patch it over with performance. You build up an exterior so impenetrable no one can catch a glimpse of the real you, the inner you. You are a beautiful house filled with shame.

Remember what Jesus called the religious perfectionists of his day? He called them "whitewashed tombs" (Matthew 23:27). He said they were perfect on the outside, but inside they were filled with rotting bones, like airbrushed corpses. Polished-up turds.

Why? Because the heart is where shame lives. And the hardest thing for perfection addicts to do is admit they need help, admit they don't have it all together. But our flaws are actually the on-ramp to freedom from shame. That's the start of second-chance living.

You may love the image you have created. But Jesus loves the mess beneath. He loves the real you. The scared you. The shame-trapped you. That's why the shell of perfectionism has to crack and fall away under the crushing weight of our own increasing standards.

And, yeah, it's no fun to crack. It feels vulnerable. It's unpleasant. It's a little like dying, but only things that die can come back to life.

Don't seek perfection. Seek goodness. Wonderful, messy, love-saturated goodness. You will find there is nothing better than the love and grace God pours into your sad, silly, sin-broken attempts at moving in his direction. In fact, you might even call it . . . *perfection.*

YOU ARE NOT A

broken thing.

YOU ARE A

healing thing.

YOU DID NOT STEP BACK;
YOU LEAPED FORWARD.→

MIKE FOSTER

Ten

Be Beloved

Dad did it faithfully every morning. He woke before the sun rose. He grabbed the morning paper from the driveway, lawn, or rat-infested ivy—wherever the paperboy had lobbed it that day. He retrieved it without complaint. He'd served in the navy, so I'm sure he had standards of excellence, but he let the paperboy's haphazard skills or blatant disregard for quality get a pass.

His routine was the same each morning. After he had retrieved the paper, he would sip down a healthy smoothie shake—and this was before smoothie shakes were cool—jump in the shower, and get ready for his hour-long drive to Los Angeles. He worked for the city bus line, helping millions of Angelenos get where they needed to go.

Before going to work, he splashed on some Brut cologne and cinched his tie. And then, in the middle of his busy morning routine, Dad made his way to the kitchen to prepare something sacred: a sack lunch for me. He didn't know it was sacred at the time, but his hands crafted a slice of heaven for me on those mornings. A sandwich, chips, a fruit cup with a plastic spoon, and always, always a little yellow note written just for me.

There is a special category of human activities: tiny greatness. Holiness in the small, unsuspecting work of our hands. A massive flow of Jesus spilling out in barely noticed actions. It's like a silent fireworks show from heaven that only angels get to see here on earth. We lowly humans just hear faint words and promptings that say, "Keep doing that. Make more of that stuff, because it's good and it matters."

If only we could hear the loud booms or sparkly explosions in these sacred moments, we wouldn't be so quick to dismiss these acts of tiny greatness. If only we could get a glimpse of heaven standing in awe, cheering like wide-eyed children on the Fourth of July when these small holy acts occur. Instead we label them as insignificant or ask, "What difference does this small action make?"

But I think we're using the wrong measuring stick for good. God measures differently, if he measures at all. He's looking at spiritual bigness. Soul impact. Tiny greatness.

How could my dad know that his morning offering to me was so sacred? How could he comprehend the impact of my lunches and his little yellow notes? Three decades later he still doesn't recognize it. Because he couldn't see into my soul. He didn't know what I believed and felt about myself and my future at that time. He had no idea how I struggled with believing I had any value.

My school years were awkward. Misaligned days of weirdness in my soul and identity. Every kid faces these feelings, but some have advantages, such as minimal acne, athletic prowess, and (if you're really lucky) good looks. Being attractive in high school is like getting a season pass to being wanted and loved. And if not loved, at least noticed. Unfortunately, none of these were gifted to my teen years.

DESPICABLE ME

Let me set the scene. I grew too fast, making me tall and skinny. My body was a pool of hormones, and no matter how hard we fight it, hormones mess up our plans for popularity. Acne of various kinds camped out on my teenage skin. Blackheads, puss balls, and even those red marks that can't decide what they want to be, so they just sit there in all their un-popable, gross-looking glory.

We know we can't really do anything about puberty except go with it and hope it doesn't destroy everything we fought so hard for in our happy childhood, like those trophies from gymnastics and the awesome watercolor paintings that our families swooned over. We want to preserve that season when we had friends who came over to our house to play without any romantic awkwardness or rivalry. This is all in jeopardy due to puberty.

Thanks, puberty, for ruining everything!

But to be honest, I was partly to blame for my nerd status. These factors are all on me:

Factor 1: I played the French horn.

My love of the *Star Wars* soundtrack led me to believe it was a good idea to take up this musical instrument. For you nongeeks out there, the French horn is featured prominently in the film's musical score and is iconic in its melancholy sound and beauty. Nerd alert!

Factor 2: I had broken teeth and wore braces.

It is one thing to wear braces as a teenager. It's another to have your two front teeth chipped and broken from a biking accident. Seriously, they looked like jagged mountain peaks. My parents, being practical, middle-class people, decided to wait to fix the front teeth until the braces came off. It took four years.

Factor 3: I rode the bus to school.

In a car-obsessed culture like Southern California's, taking the school bus was like boarding a yellow cylinder of shame. It wasn't the pickup from home that was so stigmatizing; it was the drop-off at school. When we filed off the bus, it felt like a procession of misfits, rejects, and the socially inept.

Factor 4: I was a quiet kid.

"Quiet kid" is really just code for being different. I was an outsider who thought about life a lot. I lived in an imaginary world inside my head that left me little time to figure out how the real world worked. Today my imagination works to my advantage, but back then it kept me from having many friends. I was relegated to eating lunch each day in the school library.

And this takes us back to that sack lunch my dad made each morning.

STICKY NOTES

Like my dad, I had a routine to my day. At lunchtime I escaped to the library to eat and do my homework. I would slip out the sandwich, chips, and fruit cup. These items were food for my hormonal body, but what came next—the yellow note—was food for my soul.

The notes weren't fancy or eloquent. Most sacred things aren't. The note said basically the same thing every day. Written in Dad's printed capital letters, it read:

DEAR MIKE,
I HOPE YOU HAVE A GREAT DAY AT SCHOOL.
I LOVE YOU.
DAD

The first half of the note was basic housekeeping, but the second half was new life. Reading the words "I love you" from your dad can change your world, especially when you don't feel very lovable. Those three words contain a power that can lift us from any dark place we might be in. They always have and always will. They were especially sweet to an insecure, French-horn-playing kid. They were like an anchor for my teenage soul.

I wondered if my dad knew anything about my nerd factors. If he understood the struggle of loving *Star Wars,* being an introvert, and riding the bus. He never seemed too interested in those sorts of things. He was more interested in loving his son and sending yellow lifelines into his world. He just felt compelled to remind me that I was loved by him.

I also wondered if Dad had hoped for a son who was more popular. Like my friend Mark, who was on the football team, drove a lime-green VW bug, and leveraged his Latino charisma to draw in the ladies. I wondered if Dad compared me to Mark and his accomplishments.

My gut says he never did. He just rose each morning and made lunches and wrote encouraging sticky notes.

I HOPE YOU'RE HAVING A GOOD DAY.
I LOVE YOU.
DAD

It's priceless to be loved when you feel unlovable. It's precious to be valued when life makes you feel worthless. I'm so glad his sticky notes stuck.

I believe God cares about all the things that make you feel awkward, lousy, and rejected. But frankly I think he's a lot more concerned about loving you well and sending little inconspicuous reminders of what you mean to him.

The drama, the noise, the self-loathing, and the comparison game are never the point for him. He just keeps sending the notes that he loves you right in the middle of school, work, rehab, or the ICU. I've learned that wherever life takes us, no matter what the season looks like, the words *I love you* might just be enough to get us through.

I believe our great mission is to write our own tiny yellow notes. To remind other bus nerds that they are loved and not forgotten in the libraries of our world.

Each of us knows what it's like to be on the outside. We have felt the boundaries and the labels. The thing that is most effective in snapping us out of these moments and sucking us back into community is a small, simple reminder that we are still wanted.

THE "ME" EACH OF US TRIES TO BE

All my life I have lived with two Mikes: Normal Mike and Super Mike.

Normal Mike is a mixture of whiner and dreamer, hero and zero. A people-pleasing creative nerd with a passion to share grace, eat nachos, talk about Hot Wheels, and bore people with *Star Wars* facts. He is a mash-up of morning breath and pearly whites, fear and courage, dark and light. In short, he is a mixed bag. And because Normal Mike feels so vulnerable, he prefers to hide most of the time. When things get scary (which is most of the time), he sends someone else out to do his living for him: Super Mike.

Super Mike is pretty much perfect. He is always fashionable. His house is clean. His wisdom flows like a never-ending river. He is so kind and likable, never grumpy or snappish. He never bores people with his true interests but only talks about what is hip. He is unassailable, confident, and a projection of everything Normal Mike thinks the world demands.

He is effective, likable, and entirely competent. But Super Mike requires twice the energy of Normal Mike. He squashes his own passions to pursue what others value. He covers his flaws with performance to garner love and admiration. Super Mike is an actor playing a lifetime role, always on, always changing, always playing to the audience.

Super Mike wears me out. Big time.

Telling you about my two Mikes is my way of presenting a psychological concept known as the *false self.* This self is a secondary identity most people create to protect themselves from shame and embarrassment. But this protection comes at a cost.

James Masterson observed in his book *The Search for the Real Self* that "the false self plays its deceptive role, ostensibly protecting us but doing so in a way that is programmed to keep us fearful—of being abandoned, losing support, not being able to cope on our own, not being able to *be* alone."[1]

We protect ourselves but lose ourselves. By trying to be the me others want me to be, I lose the I that I really am. I live a false life with borrowed passions. I armor my heart so nothing can touch it, but at the same time, nothing can get out.

Most of our false identities flow from a desire to be loved. Love is all we ever want in the first place, right? Our playacting is a desperate grasping for acceptance and value. It's our strategy for belonging. We wear masks and become characters in a nice story, but it's not *our* story.

It's a primary symptom of believing the lie. We become convinced that being our real selves means risking rejection and that whatever is real about us could never be as valuable as what we have manufactured. And all of this energy, work, and role-playing greatly hinders human flourishing. It makes us miserable, tired, and ineffective. It ruins our lives.

THE RECIPE FOR DESPAIR

The philosopher Søren Kierkegaard observed that all human despair is caused by people not willing to be their true selves. He called it the "sickness unto death."[2] This despair comes in three flavors: you feel like a fraud for living a lie, you feel like a coward for not being who you are, or you don't feel anything at all because you aren't even aware there is a problem.

Signs of this sickness that leads us to death are everywhere. Antidepressant usage is rising. People are self-medicating with their substances of choice. Despair is cropping up in every sector of society. Even the church.

In the last few years, researchers have surfaced a remarkable fact: the clergy are suffering from burnout en masse. One study conducted by Duke University concluded that 70 percent of pastors acknowledge their self-esteem has suffered since beginning ministry.[3] In the last decade the use of antidepressants by pastors has spiked. On a purely statistical basis, their life expectancy has fallen.[4] It happens privately and quietly, but it's inarguable. What was once a profession associated with contentment and goodwill has become, for far too many, unhealthy and unhappy.

Public health experts say there is no easy explanation. But I think I know what it is: it's that sickness that leads to death. The fear of being one's true self. Nobody feels more pressure to be perfect than the person in the pulpit.

Even our kids feel the pressure of despair. In their book *Identity Formation, Agency, and Culture,* authors James Côté and Charles Levine explain that "identity formation has changed in significant ways for many young people attempting to make their way into adulthood, so much so that we are witnessing a proliferation of identity-related problems, and even pathologies."[5] They go on to say that this identity crisis among young people is a result of modernity.

In earlier societies, people inherited a good portion of their identity from their family, tribe, or culture. Today, for the first time in history, kids have to construct their identity for themselves. They choose their occupation, mates, and values. Combine this with the always-on nature of social media, and the pressure to create a perfect false self is sky-high. Apps like Hot or Not give an instant ranking of your appearance. Views, followers, and likes assess your self-worth. Image management becomes a forty-hour-a-week job.

THE FOUNDATION OF THE BE-LOVED

So what is the answer to this exhausting work of presenting a false, others-approved version of ourselves to the world? How do we reignite our passion and begin to feel again? How do we grow our hearts and engage with the world without being overwhelmed?

We need to shift our primary identity off whatever foundation we have built and place it firmly back where it belongs. That foundation is knowing we are God's beloved.

I know that sounds a little weird. In our supercompetent, take-charge, change-the-world culture, believing our beloved status seems awfully passive. It seems to paint life as a sentimental romance movie with rolling hills and a young couple dressed in Victorian clothes gently paddling across a serene pond. "Oh, look! They are so in love. They are each other's beloved!"

Nice image, you might say, but my life is part action movie, part tragedy, and part horror flick. I have to work. I have to fight off challenges. I have things that will only get done if I do them. I have habits I need to get under control. I have passions I need to pursue. I mean, we need to tell people about Jesus! We need to get out there, save lives, save souls, fight the devil, serve the church, and change the world!

I get it. I feel all those pressures too. All those things are real. But the more I read the Bible and the more I journey along in my faith, the more I realize that no matter what you and I have made our lives about, the ultimate point of our existence is to be loved by God. It's about entering into a love relationship and enjoying him. Period. End of story.

He loves you. The real you. He wants to be with you, bless you, help you. Throw you a love party. And, no, it may not look like a scene from *Pride and Prejudice,* but it will look better than what you have now. God wants to enter your crazy, challenging, freak-show life and baptize it with his extravagant love. He wants to be with you, loving you through it all.

That's what it means to be his beloved.

I recently renewed my wedding vows with my wife, Jennifer, on the warm, breezy shores of Hawaii. As the palms swayed and my friends and family stood nearby, we looked into each other's eyes and said, "I do."

Pure magic.

What made it so special? We were not young, ignorant lovebirds eager to toss our purity bracelets in the trash. We were not caught up in the wild newness of starting a life together. We had twenty years of history under our belts. Twenty years of fights. Of secrets. Of ugliness.

We were not so bright and shiny anymore. Not so innocent. We had known each other at our utter worst and in our darkest moments. We had let each other down. Hurt each other deeply. Two decades of learning to love and be loved.

And that is what God says to us every day. To you every day. "I know who you really are, and you are my beloved." Your core identity is that of God's beloved. You are the object of his special love and favor. Your true self is a delight to him. He knows all your faults, sins, passions, and strengths, and he is crazy about you. Not like a newlywed, but like a twenty-year renewal. His love is based on knowledge, not ignorance. The one who knows you best loves you most.

Tim Keller summed up the gospel like this: "We are more sinful and flawed in ourselves than we ever dared believe, yet at the very same time we are more loved and accepted in Jesus Christ than we ever dared hope."[6]

THE MANIFESTO OF SELF-ACCEPTANCE

Before I accepted my identity as God's beloved, I was never enough. What I accomplished was never enough. And whatever good was there in front of me was impossible for me to take pleasure in, because I was trying so hard to *be* good that I couldn't just *embrace* the good.

I was always bringing a false self to God, but God can't love Super Mike. Super Mike is a figment of my imagination. So I was unable to experience God's love, and that meant I failed to see how he loved me. I had no idea who I was. And in that confusion a light dawned, dim but sure.

I knew I needed to love myself again. The real me. I need to pull Normal Mike out of his hiding place and present him to God with all his flaws, all his mistakes, all his failures, and all his cowardice and cruelty. I needed to get my prodigal self back home as my true self. I needed to feel my heavenly Father wrap his arms around the real me and say, "My son who was dead has come back to life!"

LOVE OTHERS AS YOURSELF

It can sound a little selfish and touchy-feely to say that self-love is the answer to our deepest needs. Isn't this just more positive psychology hoo-ha? Nope. We see the principle right in the words of Jesus.

When Jesus was asked to pick the greatest commandment, he actually offered up two commandments from two Old Testament scriptures and then fused them together into a one-two punch of how to live a powerful life. He said, "'You must love the LORD your God with all your heart, all your soul, and all your mind.' This is the first and greatest commandment. A second is equally important: 'Love your neighbor as yourself'" (Matthew 22:37–39).

I'm no Bible scholar, but I can't help but notice those last two words: "as yourself." In one statement Jesus links the ideas of loving God, loving your neighbor, and loving yourself. In my experience, this rings true. All three of those loves tend to rise and fall together. The more you love one, the more you love the others. People who never learn to love their true selves are often also limited in their love for God and others.

Carl Jung wrote the following in *Modern Man in Search of a Soul*:

> The acceptance of oneself is the essence of the moral problem and the epitome of a whole outlook upon life. That I feed the hungry, that I forgive an insult, that I love my enemy in the name of Christ—all these are

> undoubtedly great virtues. What I do unto the least of my brethren, that I do unto Christ. But what if I should discover that the least amongst them all, the poorest of all the beggars, the most impudent of all the offenders, the very enemy himself—that these are within me, and that I myself stand in need of the alms of my own kindness—that I myself am the enemy who must be loved—what then?[7]

What if the person you need to be kindest to is yourself? What if the enemy you need to forgive or the prisoner you need to release is your true self? That is why God redeemed you. Is the self he saved at a party or in prison? Who is holding you captive?

Remember the story of the prodigal son that I discussed earlier? The father threw a party in the son's honor, but there were a few different ways the son could have behaved at this party. These are also ways we can respond to being God's beloved.

How not to behave at a party: Be a wallflower.

There are people at every party who like to hide. They feel so self-conscious they simply cannot enjoy themselves. They prefer to lurk in the shadows rather than step out into the spotlight.

Introversion and shyness aside, when it comes to behaving this way at God's party, I think the reason is a bit more insidious. It's a feeling of dirtiness, of ugliness. You look at your past, your sin, and you simply cannot forgive yourself. You feel the party invitation was some kind of error or loophole. You must keep a low profile or risk getting thrown out. You hear you are God's beloved, but you don't really believe it. You feel like a stowaway who'll be ditched the moment you're discovered.

How not to behave at a party: Be a servant.

Some people only feel comfortable jumping up and serving at a party. They never sit. Never rest or enjoy the festivities. They spend all their time rushing from one job to another. They earn their keep and affirm their place at the party by making sure it happens for others.

I see this a lot in church. Often the people who seem most committed and most involved are enjoying God the least. True, some people are just servant hearted, but that can take a nasty turn. You start feeling like that is your payment for being saved. You must prove your worth. You can't let anyone down, most of all God! Why? Because you hear you are God's beloved, but you don't really believe it. You feel like a slave, someone who will be tossed aside if you ever stop being useful.

How not to behave at a party: Be a party pooper.

Some people just don't like parties. They prefer things quiet and solemn and routine. When cars start to fill up the street, they pound on your door and complain. When the music and laughter get too loud, they call the police. When you invite them to join in the joy, they storm off, offended, unable to feel anything but contempt for your disturbing their plans.

Even the story of the prodigal son had a party pooper. The elder brother refused to join the festivities. He tried to pawn off his offense on his father, saying, "You never threw me a party!" But it was all a smokescreen. The elder brother could have thrown a party any time he wanted, because he owned the joint! No, his real problem was that he didn't like parties. And he didn't want the love of his father. He wanted anything but that. Everything but that. He wanted what his father could get him but not what his father longed to give him: love.

What exactly do you want from God? What role are you playing at his party? I've decided to be what he wants us all to be: a guest of honor. I've spent plenty of time being a wallflower, a servant, and a party pooper. I'm fed up with it. I'm too tired. I'm not made for it. I need his love. His prodigal love served up at his prodigal party.

Did you know that the word *prodigal* does not mean "bad"? When we hear the phrase "prodigal son," most of us figure it means the boy was immoral or licentious or a runaway, but it doesn't. It means "extravagant." It means "lavishly more than what is expected or required." The prodigal son was *extravagant* in how much he hurt the father, *extravagant* in how he wasted his father's resources on pleasure. But the father was also *extravagant* in his grace and forgiveness. He was *extravagant* in throwing a party and restoring his son.

God is extravagant in the love he wants to pour out on your life. Don't be a party pooper. Be his beloved. He wants to lavish your true self with value.

THE ROLE YOU WERE BORN TO PLAY

This means you no longer have to audition for a part or wear a mask or pretend to be anything other than God's child. You already have the part. The role that you always wanted has already been granted to you. The tryouts are over, and it has been officially decided that you will play you and I will play me. The programs have been printed, and all that is required now is that you learn your lines and fully embrace every aspect of who you are. And please, please, for heaven's sake, don't play someone else. If you don't do you, the story won't go as planned.

We must return to the beginning. To the garden. To the gospel of the good news where our Creator says to each of us, "I'm glad you're mine. You are my son, my daughter. You will always be mine." No need to find yourself. You are found. No need to wear the negative labels anymore. You are labeled with love.

SEEING YOURSELF IN HIS STORIES

Part of the problem with religion is that it prevents us from seeing ourselves in the proper light. Religion has a tendency to make us approach Scripture as if we're the outsiders looking in. We're trying to find some meaning in the story. We tend to forget that the story is actually about us and God.

Instead, we're off at a distance. We peer into Jesus's life through these stories, and we think, *That's so good of him to do that. That's so nice. Isn't that nice?* What we don't realize is that we are the sheep that ran away. We are the person in prison. We are the Samaritan woman at the well.

In every instance Jesus is talking about us. And he's telling us, "This is how much I love you. Let me give you all these different examples of how I love you and people like you and people not at all like you. Let me tell you why I came here and how I'm not in favor of anything or anyone that stands in the way of your realizing how much you are loved. That includes the religious leaders. It includes people and institutions that say you're not right, that there's something wrong with you."

Some may be saying right now, "Hey, Mike, isn't part of the gospel that there is something fundamentally wrong with us?" To that question I say, you're right. Our brokenness is part of our human condition. But that's not the good news of the gospel, even though churches sometimes tend to harp on how messed up we are. The point of the story is God's love, not our mess. A lot of us have made the mistake of what journalists call "burying the lead." We lost the headline of the story and focused instead on a detail that isn't all that compelling or even that important.

Jesus says, "I love the outsider. I love the broken. I love the sinner. I love the prostitute. I love the people who are weak and make poor decisions like the prodigal son."

He presents a constant love story of how much he wants to be with us. How much he wants to redeem us and connect us back to the Father. But we don't see ourselves this way. We're too prone to see ourselves as prisoners. We are anything but.

Wouldn't it be amazing to go back to the place where we could be who we were before anyone had an opinion about what we were supposed to be? Can you imagine your life being solely defined by the extravagant love of a Father who loves you just as you are? What if we realized that every story God is communicating to us has to do with who we are and the unmistakable point of the story is that we are loved?

THE SCANDAL OF LIKING YOURSELF

So how can we do this thing of loving ourselves again? It may feel hard, and you may not know where to begin. Here are a few simple starting points. Take them for what they're worth, but I'm guessing if you start with some of this easy stuff, you will be on the right track to a new you. Here's a way to be your real self.

- Let a few people down. Let them be disappointed in you. It's good for them. It's good for you too.
- Quit serving for a month. Yep, quit something. It feels good. It breaks the chains of duty, legalism, and trying to look awesome.
- Throw a party for no reason. Why not?
- Play hooky for a day, and do what you love to do. Do that thing you've been putting off in order to take care of everyone else.

- Read that young adult vampire novel. You know you want to. Why not now?
- Sing like crazy. And sing really loud. People will think you're strange, but that's okay. The louder you sing, the more jealous they will be of how comfortable you are in your skin.
- Spend too much on flowers.
- Binge watch that HGTV show you secretly love.
- Buy that coloring book and spend some time with it—alone.
- Tell the kids you're taking a vacation from laundry so they're going to need to wear the same underwear for a couple of days. They will survive. And so will you.

This will probably feel so foreign. It might even seem impossible. Your heart will initially resist these first few steps on the long walk to learning to love yourself. But that is when you must trust in the extravagant grace of God, hold your head up high, and say, "I am his beloved. That is who I am and that is how I will live." And may you in that utterly scandalous moment know that it's completely true.

SHOW UP.
BE BRAVE.
LIVE YOUR STORY.
SMILE WHILE YOU
DO IT.

MIKE FOSTER

Eleven

Banish Fear

I'm not scared to tell you that I am a man well acquainted with fear.

If you were to walk through my house right now and look closely, you would notice signs of one of my fears. It's something that, honestly, a grown man shouldn't fess up to.

I am afraid of the dark.

I have sixteen nightlights strategically situated in my house. Little bulbs of illumination that break the darkness at night. I have nightlights in almost every plug I own. I also have them strategically placed near my Nest fire alarms. When they sense motion nearby, they emit a moonlight glow. By the way, the kids' rooms have zero nightlights. They take after their mother. She is brave.

On a trip to Las Vegas I was so scared I almost wet my pants. I mean it. Literally. I hate heights, but I'd agreed to be strapped into the Stratosphere Hotel thrill ride called the Big Shot. It's a reverse bungee ride atop a 921-foot-high platform that launches you into the sky at forty-five miles an hour while pulling four G's of force. I cried like a scared child. And I mean that literally too.

And then there was the time I had to tell my conservative, Bible-loving, God-fearing parents that I was going to launch a new ministry (XXXchurch.com) at the largest porn convention in America because I wanted those in the sex industry to feel God's radical love for them.

Jennifer and I went to my parents' house for a Sunday night family dinner. Dad barbecued some burgers. Mom had made macaroni salad. I knew they would freak out when I told them about my porn show plans.

I begged Jennifer to tell them for me. She declined. "If you wanna go to a porn show to launch your ministry, then you have to tell your parents. I'm not doing your dirty work." There was more than a touch of sass in her voice.

Dread and fear consumed the dinner experience for me until I finally got the words out. "Mom and Dad, I'm starting a ministry called XXXchurch.com, and we're launching at a porn show next month." I tried to say it as fast as I could, hoping they wouldn't notice. They noticed. The rest of the night was a blur.

My relationship with fear is a long one. I recently found a poem I wrote in fifth grade. Other students wrote of pets, clouds, and their favorite ice cream. I wrote "Don't Take Me Away." It goes like this.

> The tree that hangs over
> me at night, with the glow
> of the street lights reflecting
> on its leaves.
> It scares me as I look
> Up and stare silently at
> Its leaves.
> I believe that it's a gruesome
> And ugly monster that will

Pick me up and take me to
His dark and creepy cave.
Whenever I think of the
Monster it sends a drizzle
Of fear up my spine
But sometimes I can cast
It out of my mind, shut my
Eyes and think of beautiful
Flowers blossoming in Spring.
But when I open my eyes
I still see that tree glowing
And hanging over me thinking
It will take me away.

In case you're wondering, the tree never did take me away. Neither did any people in white coats. I didn't even have to go to therapy . . . yet.

Fear is something we all deal with. It's a normal part of the human struggle, but lately the way we experience fear has changed. And that is affecting the way we see ourselves and the future.

THE DAY FEAR CAME TO TOWN

In a small Vermont town in the 1970s, two children played in a forest clearing. A slender man with bushy eyebrows hid along the forest edge, watching them closely. He had a 16mm camera.

The four- and five-year-olds played with reckless abandon. They paid no attention to the man. They were laughing and giggling as they imitated fart noises with each other. *Phhhrt! Phhhrt!* All was caught on the grainy footage.

No, this was not a scene from a horror movie or the reenacting of an abduction on a nightly news show. This was the work of environmental psychologist Roger Hart, who studied children in natural settings.

The footage is from his film *Play and Place,* which grew out of his doctoral dissertation at Clark University. Roger wanted to film what children do when they are completely absorbed in childhood: finding bugs, pretending to fly, eating Popsicles, playing hide-and-seek. His footage gives a glimpse into the complex nature of play and how children view the world around them. It's a cool look back to a time when our lives were filled with whimsy, spontaneity, and freedom.

His research began with his own frustration about the lack of research in this area. He said in an interview, "Almost nothing was known about how children even explored the world, and then I came across a book on baboons. And I realized that we knew more about baboons' everyday behavior than we did about children's behavior outside of school."[1] So Roger set out to learn more about the lives of children.

He began working with eighty-six children from three to twelve years old. He wanted to gather data on what they did with their free time. Where did they go? What did they do? What did they experience? His goal was to create a map of childhood explorations and experiences. But Roger's real focus was their fears.

Roger asked, "Show me the places that are dangerous. Show me the places that are scary. Take me to where you're not supposed to go, and show me where that is."[2] He would follow them. Map their journey. Film them.

And as he began consolidating the data, he found something remarkable: these children had extraordinary freedom. These children could literally go anywhere they wanted. By the age of ten, "most of the kids had the run of the entire town."[3] They would play in the fields and even go to the lake that was on the outskirts of this quaint Vermont town.

Even more extraordinary was that the parents permitted it. They *allowed* their kids to run into the woods with no fear of their being abducted or worse. And remember, this was a time when there were no cell phones, no child trackers, no big-brother CCTV cameras positioned everywhere to record everything. Parents felt no stranger danger. They let their kids run and play and encouraged freedom and exploration.

A few years ago Roger decided to go back to this Vermont town. It had been forty years since his initial research, and he wanted to repeat the experiment with modern-day kids. What he found shocked him.

He asked this new generation of children the same thing—to take him to the places they considered dangerous. Roger said, "They just didn't have very far to take me, just walking around their property, really."[4] The maps that plotted the children's activities looked quite different this time. What was a huge circle of freedom back in the 1970s now was a tiny circle.

This is where you're thinking, *Well, duh, Mike! The world has changed. Don't you watch the news? The abductions. The crazies out there. The child molesters. A million things can go wrong if we don't restrict our children. Those Vermont parents are just being responsible!*

That all makes sense if the world really has gotten worse, but in this little Vermont town, not much had changed. Forty years later it was the same physically and demographically. Crime rates were the same. There were no increased dangers of any kind.

So why was there less freedom for the children? Why were parents so insistent about the kids staying close to the house? Why did Roger's maps look so different now? His conclusion was simple: fear.

Nothing had changed except people's perceptions about danger. They now had fear where there used to be none.

Roger reconnected with Andrew, one of the four-year-olds making fart noises on his first film and now a grownup with children of his own. When asked to compare his kids' childhood to his own, he replied, "I think when we were children, you know, my parents wouldn't worry if I was gone for an hour . . . or up in the woods. But here, if my girls are gone for five minutes, I start to . . . think, okay somebody could be turning around at the end of the road and—or, you know, whatever. So that makes a big difference."[5]

His fears are vague but real. The same road he walked down as a kid might now contain an abductor. The woods he explored as a child could be a haven for psychos. As a child, he might have been gone for hours, but his girls? Only minutes. The same world that was open to him for childhood exploration is now filled with phantom threats and imagined evils.

This is what fear does. It restricts freedom. It limits exploration. It turns our gift of imagination against us.

FEAR GONE WRONG

Of course, fear is a part of life, and, yes, it isn't always a bad thing. Human beings need fear to properly function in society. If you see a tiger running down the street, you should fear it. If lightning strikes nearby, put down your golf club and run like crazy. If someone says, "Would you mind watching my four kids under the age of four?" be afraid. Be very afraid.

But something has gone wrong with our fear glands. Rather than responding only to real threats, we are reacting to imagined risks. Ralph Adolphs, a professor at Caltech, notes that modern life is "constantly triggering our fear in all kinds of ways that our natural world didn't."[6] He says we have a lot of false positives when it comes to things to fear.

This hyped-up state of freaked-out-ness is doing something terrible to us. Just as it did with the kids in Vermont, fear sucks the joy and whimsy from our lives. We're afraid to explore, to risk, to do the things we are meant to do. The cost to our souls (and our kids' souls) is great.

God takes a look at our tiny maps and draws huge freedom circles on them. He says, "Go where you want. Explore. Spread out. Expand your life and influence!" But fear is always at our elbows, saying, "Yeah, but the bogeyman could be out there. You could get hurt or lost, or who knows all the terrible stuff that can go down?"

God spurs us on to greater possibilities. Fear holds us back with imaginary insecurities. The landscape hasn't changed, but our perceptions have.

Here is what I have come to see in my life. Most of the things I am scared of are really not that scary. Fear loves to multiply. Fear and worry hook up in my heart and breed like rabbits, scurrying concerns with sharp teeth and scary masks and spooky soundtracks.

But I give these creatures oxygen and fuel. I allow them space in my heart and thoughts. I provide the food and water so they can create countless worst-case scenarios. And I don't know about you, but my brain is great at creating worst-case scenarios. It gets plenty of help from the world we live in.

Frank Furedi, a sociologist at the University of Kent, studied how fear differs across cultures. Not only *what* we fear but also *how* we fear. He made a startling discovery.

In the past we experienced fear as a reaction to some object or experience. People feared death, spiders, or an impending diarrhea attack when the captain turns on the Fasten Seat Belt sign. We feared an actual thing. Now, says Furedi, fear *is* a thing. No object needed. Society can now be scared when there is nothing to be scared of.

He provides a variety of examples. One is crime. In the past, crime was seen as a byproduct of human civilization that could be contained and rarely affected most individuals. This was true. Statistically, your chances of being a victim of crime were unlikely. However, in the 1970s crime became a political issue. This increase in crime awareness caused an increase in the general anxiety and fear surrounding crime. The government responded to this fear with something called quality-of-life policing. I bet it made someone's political career.

This cultural influence is called the crime complex. We see it also in the mass marketing of burglar alarms, outdoor lights, panic rooms, and watchdogs. Those purchases may make us feel better, but according to Furedi, "Numerous surveys have indicated that often those who are most apprehensive about becoming victimized are the ones least likely to experience it."[7]

This manufacturing of fear has had dramatic social effects. Furedi contends that human beings have begun to see the species as "at best a mixed blessing and at worst wholly dangerous."[8] Rapid social changes brought about by technology cause new anxieties and new forms of panic. We have begun to view ourselves as a plague on the Earth, disrupting the natural functions of the planet and its ecosystems. This debased view of humanity results in a baseline mistrust of people.

Nothing has changed, but everything is different. We are gulping down fear by the bucketfuls.

CULTURE OF LOW EXPECTATION

This pessimistic view creates a culture of low expectation. Humanity is throwing in the towel on humanity. Watch any nature documentary, and the message is clear: human beings are a hopeless case and are destroying the planet. Watch the History Channel, and you discover we are basically a batch of evil beings who are constantly destroying ourselves. Turn on CNN and watch it happening live.

This dark view of our world is not only stoking the flames of fear, but it's also crushing our faith in the possibility of solving our own problems.

Sociologist Barry Glassner agrees that modern fear is mostly a product of the bad perception of events rather than the events themselves. This means humanity tends to move from catastrophe to catastrophe, keeping all of us on edge. In his book *The Culture of Fear: Why Americans Are Afraid of the Wrong Things,* Glassner says, "Give us a happy ending and we write a new disaster story."[9]

Glassner found a huge disparity between fears and facts. Check out some of his findings about the time period he was primarily addressing, the 1990s (it's basically the same today):

Fear: Two-thirds of us thought crime rates were soaring in the 1990s.
Fact: Crime rates plunged throughout the 1990s.

Fear: Nine out of ten adults believed the drug problem was out of control.
Fact: In the late 1990s the number of drug users had decreased by half compared to the 1980s.

Fear: Pundits warned of imminent economic disaster.
Fact: In the late 1990s the unemployment rate was below 5 percent for the first time in a quarter century.

Fear: Women in their forties believed they had a 1-in-10 chance of dying from breast cancer.
Fact: The actual risk was more like 1 in 250.

Glassner also discovered overinflated fears about child predators. "Hysteria over the ritual abuse of children cost billions of dollars in police investigations, trials, and imprisonments."[10] Across the nation, expensive surveillance programs were implemented to protect children from fiends who reside primarily in the imaginations of adults.

THE FEAR MAKERS

Glassner believes politicians, advocacy groups, and the media are chiefly responsible for overstated fears. The media, he says, are an organism that thrives on fear. They are factories of sensationalism. Every story about some new disease or some new catastrophe draws new viewers like moths to a flame. Politicians and advocacy groups warp stats so things appear more dangerous than they are. They do this to benefit their own campaigns or, in the case of advocacy groups, their financial betterment. This mass distortion of facts and statistics has had a direct effect on society and culture.

If you want to see how much this culture of fear is affecting your daily attitude, I challenge you to take a news fast. No papers, no blogs, no television. I'm willing to bet that within a week you will start to feel as though maybe things aren't so bad after all. Global conflicts that will never reach your doorstep will seem far less important than the people right in front of you. A tragedy you were never meant to hear about, and can't do anything to affect, won't steal hope and energy from the good you are called to put into the world. Fear will start to lose its grip.

The other thing we can do is fill our hearts with stories of overcomers. We need to elevate moments of togetherness and connectedness. More ice cream socials and picnics in the parks with people who aren't like you. More notes of encouragement and acts of tiny greatness. More prayer, because God is a force to be reckoned with.

And above all, a complete and total rejection of fear for its own sake. Don't cave to the fear peddlers. God is still in control of this world. And he is still in control of your world.

NOT REALLY REALITY TV

I believe that fear creates dependency, and dependency creates customers, followers, or whatever else the fear maker needs. If you are not afraid, you do not turn to the news for information that can address those fears. If you are not afraid, you do not subscribe to the inflammatory newsletter, blog, or radio show that keeps you abreast of the situation. If you are not afraid of the movie plot or television show that dredges up the worst tragedies the human mind can imagine or endure, you are not interested. If you are not interested, you do not pay attention, and then that show, news program, or blogger loses power. They can no longer make money because they do not have your eyeballs.

People go to the ends of the earth to find a shred of disaster or conflict or human tragedy or injustice and tease it into a week-long affair. And while I believe the world needs news media, and I certainly do not deny the world has problems, most of what comes at us is not designed to inform but to inflame. To keep us in a state of fear.

Why? Ultimately to sell toilet paper. Or hearing aids. Or car insurance. Seriously. Note the advertisers of your news source. That is why your attention is so valuable. I'm sure there are lots of good people involved in the news industry, people who care about truth and justice. But the system runs on fear. Because nothing gathers a crowd like fear.

SUCKER-PUNCHING FEAR

All the forces that work on our outer world also wreak havoc on our inner worlds. Fear presses on our souls to keep us from becoming who we are meant to be. In most cases our fear to change, branch out, or become our true selves is based not on facts but on our perceptions. And so the real reason we remain stuck is our own insecurity. We stay close to home, never exploring the wide-open space God gives us because, well, you know, something bad might happen.

When God calls us to risk, we usually react with fear. He says, "I want you to try this," and we freeze up. Rather than trust him, we doubt.

A great example of this kind of fear can be found in Exodus when God called Moses. God showed up in a burning bush and told this ex-prince of Egypt to expand his map of freedom. God wanted him to be a leader, a deliverer, a spokesman. Moses was to go on the adventure of his life. He was to make history. He was to be a part of God's amazing plan to rescue people!

Once Moses's head stopped spinning, the fear fog set back in. Doubts clogged his heart. He asked the three basic questions that insecurity always asks. The same questions you and I ask when God taps us for a new mission. Luckily for Moses, and us, God gave some solid answers that punched fear right in the throat.

Question 1: Who am I?

This is always our first doubt when God asks us to do something. We wonder, *Why me?* This usually has to do with doubts about our qualifications. Or maybe a better way to put it is our *dis*qualifications. We look back on our lives and see nothing but unworthiness and failure.

God resurrected a dream that Moses had in his heart long ago—to rescue the people of Israel. But he'd already tried it forty years ago and totally blown it. He'd been rejected, run out of town. He'd turned his back on his past and adopted a new, quiet life. Never mind that he used to be an Egyptian prince, that he had been miraculously delivered from a river, and that his very name meant "to draw out of." Moses glossed over those details and saw only his disqualifications.

When Moses asked, "Who am I?" God's response was "I'll be with you" (see Exodus 3:11–12). Basically he said, "Because I said so. Because you're my guy. It's not about you and your comfortable, quiet life and your past mistakes. This is about me, my plan, and other people's futures."

When we are tempted to ask the "Why me?" question, the better question is "Why not me?" God can use anyone he wants to do whatever he wants. Do you seriously think there is anything in your past that can stop his all-powerful will from accomplishing his plans?

When fear says, "Who are you?" punch it in the throat and say, "I'm God's beloved, dude! I can do whatever he tells me to do!"

Question 2: What if they . . .

Then Moses started to think about what would happen if he said yes. Fear filled his mind with all kinds of worst-case scenarios. He said, "What if they don't believe? What if they don't listen? What if it doesn't work? What if people think I'm nuts?" (see Exodus 4:1).

Isn't it amazing how quickly insecurities can shift from our past to the future? We say, "That's a cool idea, but it will never work. People won't respond. It will never get funded. I'll be a laughingstock. I won't be able to handle the pressure or demands."

When we ask the "What if they . . ." question, God responds with his own. He asks, "What is that in your hand?" (verse 2). Moses held a staff, representing his identity as a shepherd. God imbued it with his power—a sign to convince the Israelites that Moses was the real deal, representing an all-powerful God.

What is in your hand? What do you love? What are you passionate about? What breaks your heart? God has given us all the ability to do certain things well. Let these be clues to guide us from the place of safety to the place of exploration.

Question 3: What if I . . .

Moses's last concern was his competency. He actually didn't ask a question here. Instead, he begged, "O Lord, I'm not very good with words. I never have been, and I'm not now, even though you have spoken to me" (Exodus 4:10). Moses was more confident in his weakness than he was in God's strength.

I've spent a lot of time living where Moses is in this scenario. I fear my own failure more than I trust God's call. I give more respect to my inability than I do to God's sovereignty. I want to wimp out, kill my dreams, and crawl under a rock. I'd rather not try than not succeed. Maybe you do the same thing?

God got really straightforward with Moses. "Who makes a person's mouth? Who decides whether people speak or do not speak, hear or do not hear, see or do not see? Is it not I, the LORD? Now go! I will be with you as you speak, and I will instruct you in what to say" (verses 11–12).

Moses was concerned only about his stuttering mouth. He thought for sure that his weakness would mess up God's whole plan, but God told him, "Look, your mouth is the least important part. I'm handling the results; you just need to handle the obedience. Got it?"

I need to hear these words often. Other people's responses are not my responsibility. Only my response is my responsibility.

God has made us. He has made the people he wants to reach through us. He will help us do what needs to be done. He will manage how our work is received. So stop worrying. Stop wondering. Fear not.

Or in the words of God, "Now go!" Adventure awaits.

DON'T LET A
moment
OF *pain*
CUT YOU OFF
FROM A *lifetime*
OF *grace*.

MIKE FOSTER

Twelve

Move from Bad Story to Backstory

I used to love Saturday morning cartoons. Each weekend I woke up early, toasted some Pop-Tarts, and plopped myself in front of the television for four sweet, sweet hours of animated entertainment. This childhood tradition has evaporated with the onslaught of cable channels, Redbox, and Netflix, but back in the 1970s, Saturday morning was a high and holy time.

One of my favorite shows was called *Super Friends.* It was like a hipster version of the Avengers. (They were a team of heroes before that was cool.) Superman, Batman, Robin, Wonder Woman, Aquaman, and others gathered at the Justice League to take down whatever villain of the week was hatching a plan for world domination.

My all-time favorite heroes were called the Wonder Twins. When this brother-sister team fist-bumped, they could shape-shift into whatever they wanted. I always thought it would be rad to become an eighteen-wheeler, because my other favorite show was *B. J. and the Bear,* a trucker comedy. I also liked that the twins had to work together. Their superpowers only worked when they touched hands. Kind of like our gifts as Christ followers (but more on that later).

This decade has seen an explosion of superhero movies that are crushing it at the box office. We apparently love stories about people who have special powers, who are extrastrong or extrasmart, who have skills and gear and enhanced senses. What's better than munching buttery popcorn while the Hulk smashes, Wolverine slashes, or Captain America puts the hurt on bad guys with his adamantium shield?

It's a lot of fun to see the spectacular action in superhero films, but what really gets our hearts involved is not the fight scenes. It's the origin stories. A radioactive spider bites Peter Parker, and Parker becomes Spider-Man. Natasha Romanova is an orphaned Russian girl who is brainwashed by the government and transformed into a professional killer called Black Widow. Tony Stark is wounded in an explosion and taken prisoner, builds a suit to save his life, and escapes as Iron Man.

In each case a normal person is transformed into a hero by the tragic events of his or her past. We are attracted by their strengths, but we connect with their weaknesses.

I don't think it's accidental that we find such a story line so compelling. I think it's the way God works in our lives. He takes the hard things of our past—the losses, failures, and betrayals—and he turns them into our unfair advantage.

So what is *your* backstory? What tragedy from your past is fighting to become a strength in your future? What old wounds give you the tenderness and authority to be someone's hero?

We tend to think of our heartbreaks as setbacks. As mistakes and failures. We look back on the foolishness, sinfulness, and pride of our past and think it was all a waste of time. But God doesn't just redeem our future; he redeems our whole lives. He bends every experience we've had, the dark and the light, toward the good things he is bringing about in our lives and in the world.

He's just awesome that way. He takes your bad story and makes it your backstory. It becomes the interesting tale of how you got your superpowers. People are attracted to the gifts that make you strong, but they are positively affected by the hurts that make you human.

HEALED TO BE HEROES

The best Bible passage I know to describe the way God uses our broken past to help others heal is 2 Corinthians 1:3–5: "All praise to God, the Father of our Lord Jesus Christ. God is our merciful Father and the source of all comfort. He comforts us in all our troubles so that we can comfort others. When they are troubled, we will be able to give them the same comfort God has given us. For the more we suffer for Christ, the more God will shower us with his comfort through Christ."

Did you catch that? When we suffer, God *himself* comforts us. Then, with his support, we come alongside others to comfort them. That's the way the Christian life works. He heals us so we can be heroes. He gives us an unfair advantage.

Your past does not disqualify you from having a huge impact on others. Your failures do not rob you of authority. Your losses do not make you weak. Your frustrated passions do not make you foolish. Quite the contrary. When you surrender those little deaths to God and walk with him through the darkness, he not only brings you out on the other side, but he also breathes new life into your soul.

Your checkered past is now an asset. Your failures resurface as wisdom. Your losses make you stronger. Your passion becomes a reliable guide. God uses broken things to make other broken things beautiful again.

This idea took a long time to sink in for me. It wasn't easy for me to believe it. The common narrative we're force-fed all day and every day is that it's way better to be beautiful, talented, and popular. We think unfair advantages are something people are born with. Some people win the genetic lottery. Most don't.

This perception starts around junior high and continues through high school. Every campus has its cool crowd. The popular kids. That savvy clique of demigods who wear the best clothes, excel at sports, have great hair, get invited to all the parties, and basically live the good life while the rest of us look on in wonder. They have all the fun, but we have all the struggles. It's seems so unfair.

But according to a ten-year study by the University of Virginia, these natural-born advantages don't last as long as we think. In fact, they can turn into weaknesses.

Researchers found that teens who were romantically involved at an early age, engaged in delinquent activity, and placed a premium on hanging out with physically attractive peers were thought to be popular by their peers at age thirteen. But over time this sentiment faded. By twenty-two, those once-cool teens were rated by their peers as being less competent in managing social relationships. They were also more likely to have had significant problems with alcohol and drugs and to have engaged in criminal activities.

Joseph Allen, the lead researcher, concluded, "It appears that while so-called 'cool' teens' behavior might have been linked to early popularity, over time, these teens needed more and more extreme behaviors to try to appear cool, at least to a subgroup of other teens."[1]

Apparently, winning the genetic lottery makes you too cool for school but ill equipped for life.

Another study found that a pitiful love life actually boosts your high school GPA by almost half a grade. According to University of Southern California professor Andrew Hill, boys who have only a few female friends and girls who know only a few boys are much more likely to do well during their high school years. Students in the research who experienced "'trouble paying attention in class' and 'trouble getting along with the teacher' were also more likely to have lots of friends of the opposite sex."[2]

Listen, I'm not saying you should be happy that you never went on dates in high school or should celebrate that you felt like a reject. Instead, I'm saying that actual facts push back on the cultural narrative that good looks are everything and your love life is a measure of your worth as a human being. I'm calling into question the idea that happiness is a cocktail of good looks, hot sex, and no problems.

Success and popularity may be celebrated in our culture, but they are not the qualities that produce heroes. What we miss sometimes is that those we would put in the success category have fought many battles in their own lives. Character is formed through adversity and overcoming. Happiness is not something only lucky people get; it's a byproduct of becoming who you were meant to be.

God has given you an unfair advantage, and it's most likely hidden in the darkest part of your story. Birthed not in your strengths but in your brokenness.

FINDING YOUR UNFAIR ADVANTAGE

With all my heart I believe that a brilliant diamond is buried in the earth of our fears, insecurities, and efforts to prove ourselves worthy. The diamond is there, I repeat. It's just waiting to be unearthed.

Finding it requires us to search the darker places of our stories. Places we would rather not look. The years we drank too much and traded our family for a bottle of Jack Daniel's. The mistake of trusting people who weren't trustworthy, so they took things that were important to us. Friends who loved us until they decided we weren't worth it. The moments when our worst nightmares became reality. Losing the house. Losing our innocence. Losing our kids. Losing our dignity. It is in those deep, dark places that we find diamonds.

But diamonds don't just show themselves to us. We have to dig in the dirt. We sweat. We cringe. We gasp for air, doing the hard work of clearing away the mud, gravel, and clay that encase the precious things that need to come to light. It's dirty work that sometimes looks offensive to our friends, family, and unbroken people.

The diamond will come, though. Jesus taught that we will find it if we search. If we knock, doors will be opened (see Luke 11:9). So take your shovel and dig. Bang on that door. And in the unexplored depths of painful places, you will discover your unfair advantage.

And you will be confused.

Diamonds do not look like diamonds at first. You will wonder if this is actually it, because it doesn't look beautiful. It doesn't look strong. It looks as black as the night and as dirty as the earth. It smells of failure, rejection, abuse, shame, and everything you wanted to leave behind. Not precious, but worthless.

And it's true. Diamonds are just rocks until they meet the skill of a jeweler. But when you offer your brokenness to the Master Artist, the same Creator who made the stars begins to remake your diamond. The one who invented shine and sparkle takes your raw lump of compressed blackness and starts to cut with perfect strokes. He delivers blows at just the right places, grinds away all the stuff that keeps the light from passing through, and polishes it to make it shine like a star. He takes what was buried and makes it priceless. He makes broken things beautiful again.

Muscles are like that. They don't get bigger without first tearing and healing. Our hearts follow the same pattern. We are strongest where we are most broken, torn, and healed.

So think of your not-so-perfect, kinda-messy, kinda-broken story right now. What unfair advantage has God given you by your going through what you've gone through? Any frustrated plans or undone dreams? Have you learned anything from walking through the shadow of death?

Here is what I believe with all my heart: broken things can make broken things beautiful again.

Chuck Palahniuk said, "Yes, terrible things happen, but sometimes those terrible things—they save you."[3] And I would add that once the terrible things save you, you can use them to save others. So let's talk about what this looks like in practice.

WHERE IS MY SUPER SUIT?

In the movie *The Incredibles* a killer robot tears up the city. A superhero named Frozone, voiced by Samuel L. Jackson, decides he needs to come out of retirement and do something about this. While mayhem erupts around him, he yells to his wife, "Honey? . . . Where's my super suit?"

"What?"

"Where—is—my—super—suit?"

"I, uh, put it away."

A helicopter explodes outside. Meanwhile, inside, the argument becomes heated.

Frozone wants to be a hero again, but his wife has other plans. She yells, "Uh-uh! Don't you think about running off doing no daring-do. We've been planning this dinner for two months!"

"The public is in danger!" Frozone says.

"My evening's in danger!" his wife replies.

"You tell me where my suit is, woman! We are talking about the greater good!"

"'Greater good'? I am your wife! I'm the greatest *good* you are ever gonna get!"[4]

All of us want to be heroes, but we have to fight off the forces that want things to stay as they are.

In her powerful book *Between the Dark and the Daylight,* Joan Chittister explores specific ways that suffering has produced strength in her life:

> There is a light in us that only darkness itself can illuminate. It is the glowing calm that comes over us when we finally surrender to the ultimate truth of creation: that there is a God and we are not it. . . .
>
> Only the experience of our own darkness gives us the light we need to be of help to others whose journey into the dark spots of life is only just beginning.[5]

So let's take a look at some unexpected places we can find our super suits.

Addiction: the power of surrender

No one knows powerlessness like an addict. If you are an addict, you have seen how a substance or experience can take everything away, and the only way to beat this monster is to admit your own helplessness. It's in this place that God shows you how complete surrender is the only thing that truly sets us free.

The gift of addiction is that we are forced to come to the end of ourselves. Addiction takes us not just to rock bottom but even deeper. It drops us into an even-lower chamber, or perhaps it's a classroom. And in this classroom we learn the most painful truth about our lives. On the chalkboard in big, bold letters are these five words: You are not in control.

Many never visit this classroom and thus miss the beautiful lesson. They gradually have control chipped away. It is a slow torture that comes with the illusion of control. But addicts jump all the way in. They go to full-blown powerlessness and realize they must lose themselves to find themselves. An addict knows what it means to be lost, and thus an addict knows the rich blessing of what it means to be found. No one can speak of what a prodigal party really feels like better than an addict who has hit rock bottom and has a PhD in surrender.

Doubt: the power of faith

Have you ever wondered if God was there? Have there been seasons when nothing made sense? When your story was filled with questions and doubts? If you have, then you are lucky.

Many people think doubt and faith are opposite forces, but that is not true. They are complementary. Doubt causes us to examine what we really know and believe. It drives us to clarify what is true and real versus what is popular or simply passed down to us. People who pass through periods of the greatest doubt emerge with the greatest proof and assurance of who God is and how life works. They are champions of faith.

Emptiness: the power of self-care

When people lose passion in life or end up burned out, they have to deal with some deep issues of the soul. They confront their obsessive desire for good things or misplaced hunger for achievement by ending up empty and exhausted. They learn that happiness is not found in gratification or achievement but in God alone. They alone can teach the power of self-care, with the love of God as the primary source.

Loss: the power of appreciation

People who have experienced great loss—whether through the death of a loved one, the loss of health, the loss of a resource or ability, or the loss of anything deeply valued—understand like no one else the fleeting nature of life. They learn that all things must be appreciated in the present. They can teach us a healthy respect for the power of now.

Desperation: the power of weakness

We walk through some situations where everything is ripped out of our control. Suddenly our destiny, our loved ones, our futures, our hopes are in the hands of someone or something else. The illusion of our power to keep things as they are is utterly shattered. It is then we learn what it means to trust God. To be truly weak so he may be strong.

Those who walk the path of desperation learn that true power comes from resting in God and seeking out others. Christine Caine put it like this in a tweet: "When you need a miracle you'll do things you said you'd never do & go to places & people you never thought you would. Desperation is a gift!"[6]

Loneliness: the power of engagement

When we find ourselves in a season of chronic aloneness and disconnection, where relationships are not a default option in life, this invites us to be more than our social life. What we learn in loneliness is that everybody needs somebody. It also drives us to ask the question "Who needs me?" And to seek that person.

Loneliness helps us find fresh ways to be alive. Dag Hammarskjöld said, "Pray that your loneliness may spur you into finding something to live for, great enough to die for."[7] You not only learn to be with yourself; you learn how to engage.

Confusion: the power of creativity

When everything is clear and makes sense, life may be easy, but it also gets boring. It's like painting the same portrait over and over or being asked the same question every day. But when life throws us for a loop, resources dry up, or things don't work as they used to, then our questions change. The old answers don't work. This might end the administrator in us, but it revives the artist. We are often most alive when we are confronting new challenges and constructing new ways of living. People who walk through the valley of confusion come out wearing the super suit of creativity.

This is not an exhaustive list. It's not what happens to us every time. It's not a reduction of the pain we feel. It's simply a map of where we might find our super suits. It's a dream of how God might use our bad for the greater good.

THE UPSIDE-DOWN GOD

I don't blame you if your head is spinning right now. Suffering is one of those things we have a hard time understanding. The experience is so powerful, so consuming that it's hard to see it as anything other than negative, anything of eternal worth. It seems to come at us with its own truth: There is no good in this. Nor will there ever be. It's just terrible. Period.

There is just one problem with that thinking. It backs God into a corner. To quote Johnny Castle from *Dirty Dancing,* "Nobody puts Baby in a corner."[8] You can't put God in a corner. He won't fit, and even if he did, he wouldn't stay.

When you say God can't use your suffering, you place suffering above God. But our God is the upside-down God. He turns things on their heads, even the bad things that happen to us.

Keeping that truth in front of me is key to soaking in the true essence of life. It helps me to know I am not in control. It gives me permission to trust that many of the ideas I accept as true may not be. Mostly, it allows me to think of life with God as a wild concoction of joy, surprise, whimsy, and weirdness.

In the past I have given descriptions of God with authority. More and more, though, I have come to realize that it's hard to describe the mystery. So these days I say much less about what I know about God. I've grown skeptical of the God experts.

I know God is love, and I know he is with me. I know that he wants relationship. He likes to party. He is weird sometimes. I know those things to be true. Beyond those basics, I step into more questions than facts.

But as we're living on this planet, we must never forget that God doesn't always make sense to us. We can't get all of him in our heads at once. Our best hope is to get our heads into a little bit of him from time to time.

We also need to remember that life doesn't really make that much sense either. At least not looking forward. Sometimes we see a pattern looking back.

Probably one of the most surprising things about life and God is how our brokenness can be so beautiful. It took me a long time to see this truth, but once I discovered it, my life couldn't be the same afterward.

God's weirdness and upside-down-ness make life a lot more fun these days. One of the greatest joys I have is inviting this trueness of God into all our lives. Telling my friends that our failures are freedom. That our betrayals are portals to wisdom. Our pain is purifying. I love to talk about it. And write about it. And wrestle with these ideas with friends.

My favorite times are when we gather on my patio and share about the upside-down-ness of God. He is full of opposites. He is the cosmic opposite. All I have to do is look into the man-made systems and institutions and the power players of our society and say, “Yep, he certainly is different than that.” All I have to do is look at what the television news says matters, and I know he is different. I just have to look at our fascination with excess, self-promotion, violence, racism, and the growing divisions between people and wonder if God chuckles at our feebleness and our systems.

Compared to what we see elevated in our society, God is the awesome opposite in the universe. The Sermon on the Mount comes to mind.

God seems to be more like those crazy people who, in the middle of winter when it’s twenty degrees outside, strip down to their swimsuits and go for a swim in Lake Michigan, just for the fun of it. Collective wisdom says swimming is for the summertime, when the sun is shining and we have our beach bodies ready. Why would you go swimming in Lake Michigan in winter? I don’t know. It doesn’t make sense.

God does wacky and opposite things like this too. He uses our hesitations to make us heroes. He uses our brokenness to put others back together. He uses our darkness to bring others light.

CACTUS HUGGERS UNITE

A few years back Robert Downey Jr., the actor who plays Iron Man, received an award. All of Hollywood was there—the beautiful, the powerful, the cool kids.

Downey had been allowed to pick the person to present his award, but he made an unpopular choice: Mel Gibson, a guy whose addictions and failures had been put on display so the whole world could see him at his worst. The press was against him. The public disliked him. But Robert Downey Jr., in what was supposed to be his moment of glory, stood up for Mel and said:

> When I couldn't get sober, he told me not to give up hope and encouraged me to find my faith. . . . I couldn't get hired, so he cast me in the lead of a movie that was actually developed for him. . . . Most importantly he said if I accepted responsibility for my wrongdoing and embraced that part of my soul that was ugly—hugging the cactus he calls it— . . . I'd become a man.
>
> I did and it worked. All he asked in return was that someday I help the next guy in some small way. It's reasonable to assume at the time he didn't imagine the next guy would be him or that someday was tonight. So anyway on this special occasion . . . I would ask that you join me . . . in forgiving my friend his trespasses and offering him the same clean slate you have me. . . . He's hugged the cactus long enough.[9]

That is what we are born to do—become wounded healers. We use our past brokenness to participate in the redemption of others.

Life is messy, hard, and weird. We don't have to act surprised anymore.

Mike Foster

Conclusion

New Endings

I believe faith makes all things possible and love makes all things sweeter. I am a living example that God is for you. I am living proof that change is probable and that no matter what our stories look like, they matter a lot.

I never thought my boating accident could matter in a positive way, but it did.

I never believed my struggle with my own identity would help, but it did.

I never thought the shame of my childhood would bring hope, but it did.

You and I were created to be free and to embrace the undeniable fact that we are God's beloved. And now it comes to a choice we must make every day to live as his beloved and join in the work of loving others.

HAWKS WHO SEEM LIKE CHICKENS

I know a pastor who once worked at the Los Angeles Zoo. He tells a story about fifteen red-tailed hawks that were kept in a back room and never went on display. It seemed weird to him that such majestic creatures were kept hidden, so he did some poking around. He learned the birds were evidence in some mostly defunct poaching cases, and due to legal red tape, the red-tailed hawks would most likely die in captivity.

He thought that was pretty tragic. So one day he "accidentally" left their cage door open next to an open window. Then he sneaked off, imagining these masters of flight bolting into the California sky, screeching in victory as if to say, "See ya, suckahs! I'm free at last!"

He came back fifteen minutes later and was shocked to see all the hawks were still in their cage. No bolting. No screeching. Just sitting.

He charged the cage, waving his arms, trying to scare the hawks into the sky. But all they did was scatter a few feet away from him. The birds sat on the ground and looked longingly at their cage.

So he started shouting, "Don't you see the sky? That's what you're meant for! You're not chickens! You are majestic birds of prey! Go fulfill your God-given purpose!"

But the comfort of the cage was stronger than the call of the sky. None of the red-tailed hawks flew off. He had to herd them all back into the cage like goats and lock the door.

The hawks had gotten so used to cage life that they had forgotten what it was to be free. They traded purpose for predictability. And the same can happen to us.

We forget that Jesus didn't die just to save us from our sins. He came to raise us up to a brand-new life. A life free from worry, fear, shame, and condemnation. A life where God's power lives in us and works through us in all things.

Somewhere along the line we have lost sight of what freedom is. Remember, whoever defines the terms wins. What is freedom?

Is it the ability to do whatever we want, or is it the ability to become who we truly desire to be?

The Scriptures say it brilliantly: "It is absolutely clear that God has called you to a free life. Just make sure that you don't use this freedom as an excuse to do whatever you want to do and destroy your freedom. Rather, use your freedom to serve one another in love; that's how freedom grows" (Galatians 5:13, MSG).

Freedom means allowing your past to shape your future yet not control it. It's an open door to the extraordinary life you are meant for.

Sometimes I feel as if God is charging our cage, saying, "Fly! Be free!" He thinks a lot more of us than we think of ourselves. In fact, I pulled together a series of "You are . . ." statements from the New Testament. This is who God says you are:

> "You are my friends." (John 15:15)
>
> "You are the salt of the earth and the light of the world." (See Matthew 5:13–14.)
>
> "You are a chosen people." (1 Peter 2:9)
>
> "You are made right with God." (See Galatians 2:16.)
>
> "You are God's masterpiece." (See Ephesians 2:10.)

Maybe you have been told your whole life that you are useless. That's not what God says. You may think you are a nobody, but hear what God is saying about it:

> I'll call nobodies and make them somebodies;
> 	I'll call the unloved and make them beloved.

In the place where they yelled out, "You're nobody!"
they're calling you "God's living children."
(Romans 9:25–26, MSG)

No matter how enslaved, unknown, and unloved you feel (by your own choices or the choices of others), you are completely loved, completely known, and completely free. You are God's somebody. You are the beautiful beloved. He is rushing toward your open cage and yelling, "There's the sky! That's what you are meant for. Fly! Be free! Be who you are meant to be!"

STANDING RIGHT NEXT TO YOU

A few months ago my wife and I took our kids to Disneyland for a family getaway. In order to make the day extraspecial, I booked a night at the Grand Californian Hotel, which is on the Disneyland property.

So after our long day at the happiest place on the planet, the Foster family made our way back to our hotel room. We walked into the lobby and headed for the elevators. The elevator doors opened, and we stepped in with another couple. We were looking forward to taking a load off and recovering from an exhaustingly fun day at the park.

Since I had hopped into the elevator last, I was facing the back of the elevator while everyone else was facing the front, staring at the doors and the lighted numbers that illuminated as the elevator climbed higher. I looked at my kids staring at their cell phones. I glanced at my wife, who looked cute beneath her Mickey Mouse ears. And then I glanced at the other couple in the elevator with us. And this is where the story gets really interesting.

The guy was tall and slim with peppery-gray hair and a nice smile. He wore flip-flops and had a camera hanging from his neck.

And then I looked at the woman standing at his side, and I could not believe my eyes.

This woman who had stepped into the elevator was not just any Disneyland tourist going to her hotel room. She was Sandra Bullock. Yes! Academy Award–winner Sandra Bullock. And she and I were so close I could hear her breathing. Oxygen in, carbon dioxide out. Oxygen in, carbon dioxide out. I thought it was spectacular that I could hear Sandra Bullock breathing.

I looked at her tired eyes, her uncombed hair, and her slightly disheveled appearance. Although this was definitely her, at the moment she didn't look like a movie star. I guess that is what twelve hours at Disneyland will do even to famous people. It dulls the glow and aura.

Some of my favorite movies are Sandra Bullock movies. *The Blind Side. Speed. Gravity.* I actually saw *Gravity* twice in a theater, and I never do that.

So at this point I did my best to contain my fanboy emotions as I basked in the aura of an elite Hollywood actress. And I was thinking, *This is going to be the Foster family's greatest moment ever!* Our family was getting a private, exclusive elevator ride with one of the most famous people in the universe. This surely would become a moment the four of us would never forget.

The only problem was that Jennifer and the kids were oblivious to the fact that Sandra Bullock was in the elevator and standing right next to us. My wife was just staring at the elevator doors, watching the floor numbers light up, and my kids were still staring at their cell phones.

So I tried to get their attention. Big, obvious eye gestures. Hard, glaring stares at Jennifer and the kids, hoping they would get the hint. I added some slight head bobs in the direction of the celebrity.

No response.

I was beginning to quietly scream inside my head, *"Jennifer! Kids! Please, please, please look. Don't miss this moment, guys. This is absolutely awesome. Please look up from your cell phones! Looook! For crying out loud, just notice Sandra Bullock, who is standing right next to you."*

Still no response.

Well, I'm guessing at this point you probably know what happened next. Absolutely nothing. The doors to the elevator opened, and my family and I got out and began to walk to our room. The other couple stayed on the elevator, the elevator doors slowly closed, and the Foster family's most epic Disney moment passed into history.

I looked at my beloved family and asked them as calmly as I could, "Hey, guys, did you by any chance see who was on the elevator with us just now?"

They answered, "No. Who was on the elevator?"

I replied with a cool, semicalm, semifurious "I'll tell you who was on the elevator with us. It was Sandra Stinkin' Bullock, and you totally missed it!"

Then they started to scream. "Noooooooooo! You're kidding me, right? Noooooo! We were with Sandra?"

"Yes, you were! Right there! You could have actually touched her and heard her breathe if you wanted to. But you missed it."

"Why didn't you say something?" they asked.

"I tried like crazy to get your attention, but you just checked out or something or were too busy looking at your cell phones."

The shock and disappointment came pouring out of them. It was as if someone had killed the family dog and Santa had skipped our house on Christmas, all rolled into one. To this day the regret is still a touchy subject in our family.

So you may be asking right now, *Why is Mike telling me this story? What does an elevator ride with Sandra Bullock have to do with anything?*

Well, here's why. I believe your awesome second-chance life is standing next to you right now. It is so near that if you listen really, really closely, you can hear it breathing. It is all around you, and it will totally blow your mind if you simply look around and pay attention. If you reach out to grab it and enjoy the blessings of this new way of living out your story.

IT'S GO TIME

Everything in your life is a reflection of the choices you have made and what you believe about second chances. You will live out each day what you truly believe about God's grace. Your life won't lie about what is in your heart.

So my prayer is that you grab life and say, "Let's go!" No matter where you are right now, no matter what you've been through, no matter the challenges you face, live in the promises and possibilities that God offers. Don't be so exhausted or distracted by your hurts and hang-ups that you miss the epic moments standing right next to you.

Brené Brown observed, "When we deny the story, it defines us. When we own the story, we can write a brave new ending."[1]

You are free to be the beloved. Your purpose is to love. You are meant for the sky, but the choice to fly rests with you.

TIPS, DOODLES, AND STEPS TO HELP YOU RISE GLORIOUS

IT STARTS OFF HARD

Change is hard. Don't let anyone tell you differently. But knowing this can help you prepare for success. There's no need to pretend that this will be easy.

You will stumble and fumble your way into new living. People will judge you. You will get frustrated with your progress. You will have a bad day here and there. Just plan on it; it's part of the journey.

Your desire to change will create a lot of discomfort at the beginning. But it will get easier. And then, my friends, it gets *really, really* natural!

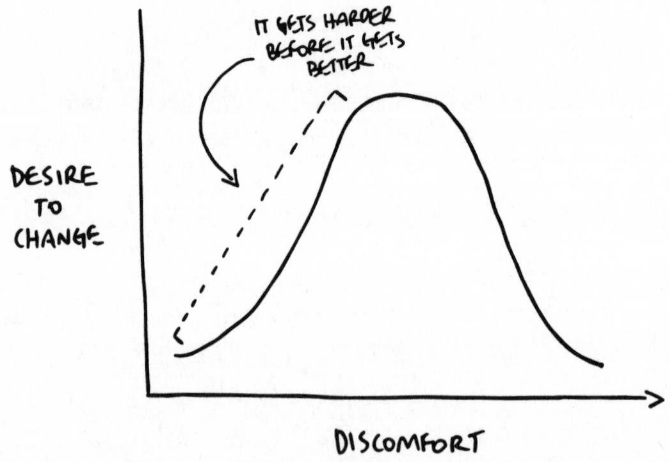

LOVE YOUR NOW LIFE!

Author Lewis B. Smedes shares in his book *Shame and Grace* that being hyperpast or hyperfuture focused undermines our opportunities in today. When we live with a hyperpast focus we become "romantics" or "victims." Romantics long for the "glory days" of life. They're stuck reliving a happy season from their past. Victims get stuck in the past by letting that event be the defining theme in their lives.

Hyperfuture people are "planners" or "after-lifers." Planners will delay life until they retire or have enough money, time, or resources. After-lifers are overly focused on heaven. For them, this life on earth is just a waiting game.

Rising glorious means we live in the here and now. We appropriately integrate both the past and the future into today's story. That's the sweet spot.

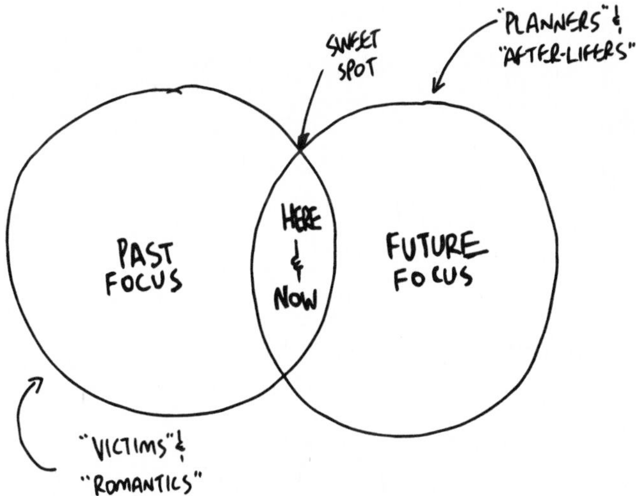

THE FORMULA

Brand this idea on your mind. Tattoo it on your heart. This is the most important thing you could remember as you begin to rise glorious. The formula for your life change is this: Love + Time = Transformation. It will always take longer than you thought and will require more love than you could ever imagine.

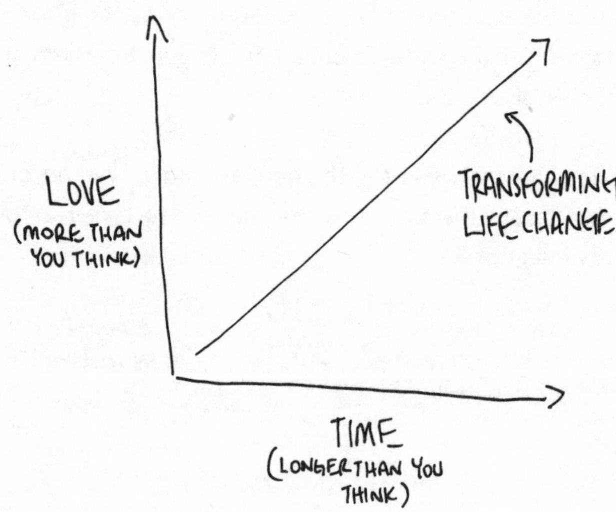

PROCESSING EMOTIONS

We often forget that as human beings we are more emotional than rational. It's how God has wired us. Many of us act more like *Star Trek*'s Captain Kirk than Mr. Spock. Pay attention to your emotions. Figure out what is causing them. Process them in a healthy way. And most of all, give yourself grace when you fail to act in a rational way.

If you identify more with Mr. Spock, it is important to understand that your emotions matter too. Give yourself permission to feel things deeply. Don't make the mistake of bottling them up or stuffing them down. Process your emotions; don't bury them.

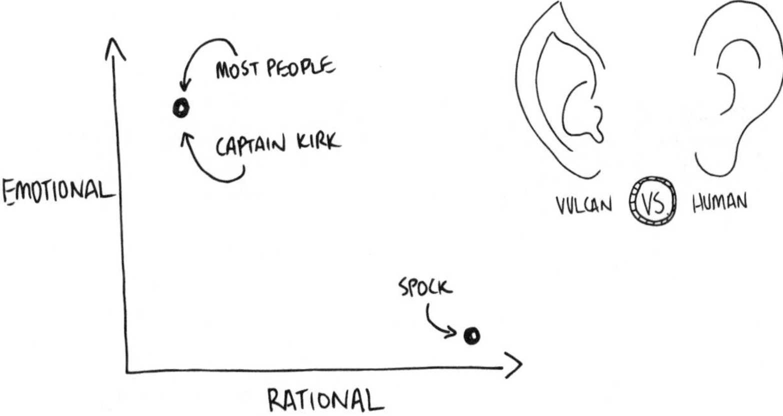

SCARS ARE BEAUTIFUL

Trauma creates wounds. Wounds create scars. The scars from our stories are very important. They can make us powerful and strong and give us our unfair advantage in life. They can also be the catalyst for hiding or pretending and the fuel to allow shame to fester and grow. Your scars are beautiful. They matter more than you might realize. Don't cover them; let them help you rise.

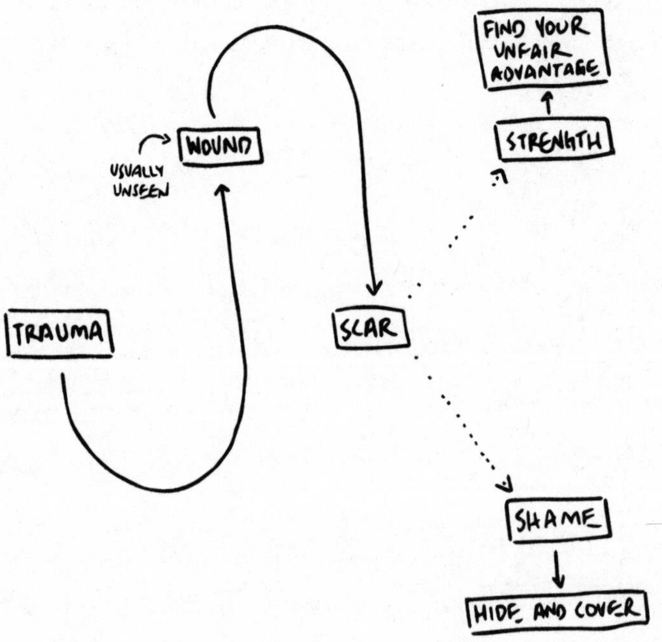

HOPE SPECTRUM

As you read the descriptions below, consider where you or your friends might fall on this spectrum.

Hurt: I am defined by my pain. I am powerless. My life's weather pattern is always cloudy and overcast. My conversations revolve around how life is unfair and hard.

Hype: I project that everything is perfect. I only show strength and share my successes. It all looks good in my life. However, deep inside I know it's not.

Hope: This is the messy middle. We integrate both our weaknesses and our strengths. Our dark and light. We live authentically with who we really are.

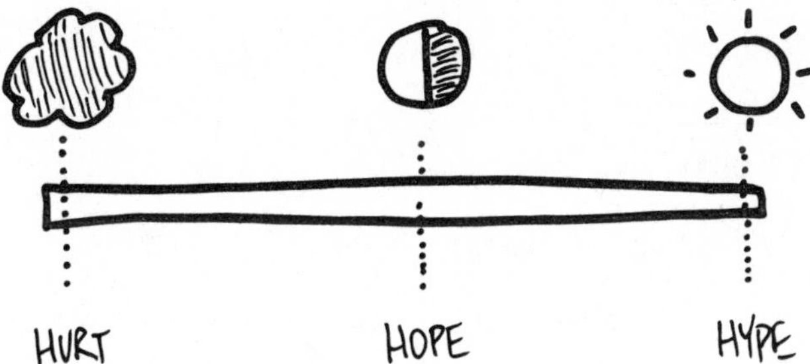

FOUR STEPS TO RISE GLORIOUS

For years I have been obsessed with how we can be fully alive in our stories. I have gobbled up countless books. I have read almost all the research. I have then applied these different techniques and strategies to my own story of struggle. I learned what worked and what didn't.

Here's basically what I found: there is no perfect solution. Unfortunately, freedom is not a plug-and-play kinda thing. There is no one answer, technique, or process that fixes everything. I wish there was, but I have yet to find it.

However, I do believe there are basic building blocks that help us deal with our broken stuff. In these next few pages, I want to share with you four steps that have really helped me and those I coach. I have also included some questions to help you reflect on your own life.

If you want to learn more about this four-step process, I recommend the "You Rise Glorious" e-course. You can access this online course free at my website:

MikeFoster.tv/rise

STEP 1:

COMPASSIONATE CURIOSITY

Ask a better question about your life.

It is in the horribleness of life that we are forced to actually examine our stories. Pain obliterates easy answers, cliches, and false beliefs. It is in these rock-bottom moments that we are invited to investigate.

In this first step, you must become curious about your life, values, and beliefs. You have to ask a better question about your story and what it all means. You must take a curious and compassionate field trip into your heart. Compassionate curiousity will lead to discovery and to finding something beautiful inside of you. You might also stumble over some long-held habits and beliefs that need to be addressed and maybe even changed. Treat it all with grace.

REFLECTIVE QUESTIONS:

Am I happy with my current reality? Explain.

If you took a field trip into your heart, what might you find?

What questions have you been allowing to define your story?

What's a bigger and better question you could ask about yourself?

STEP 2:

RADICAL ACCEPTANCE

Everything is welcomed. Everything belongs.

What if all the pain, loss, mistakes, hurt, and heartache are supposed to belong in the story of you. What if they weren't a mistake but an invitation. I call this the "theology of what is," and this belief system spends no effort on trying to fix the unfixable. It invites us into a new relationship with our pain. People who rise glorious don't run away from pain but run straight into it in order to arrive on the other side. They accept it and welcome it.

Radical acceptance means seeing everything as a lesson. Everything that has happened in your past is an opportunity to learn something. But the most important part of this step is learning to radically accept yourself. You will either love yourself or fight against yourself. Welcome every flaw, imperfection, stain, and scar. They look good on you. Remember, your scars are beautiful.

REFLECTIVE QUESTIONS:

What's one thing from your past that you think about too much?

What part of your story have you withheld from love? Why? How does this benefit you?

What one flaw could you welcome right now? How might it fit into the story God is writing in your life?

STEP 3:

RADICAL OWNERSHIP

You are more in charge than you realize.

The Enemy of your life has a basic strategy. He wants you to feel powerless. However, as I look at the teachings of Jesus, I see only a faith that empowers responsibility and choice.

Here's my basic basic belief: If you want to change, you can. If you want to stay the same, you can do that too. However, the choice is always 1000 percent yours. One choice leads to you rising glorious. The other to a life of regret and blame.

Radical responsibility says this is my story. I am ridiculously in charge of it. I don't need permission to thrive and be free. Let's build a beautifully imperferct life with no regrets!

REFLECTIVE QUESTIONS:

Is there someone to whom you have given too much power and responsibility?

What was the benefit of giving someone else the power?

What's one step you could take toward reclaiming ownership?

STEP 4:

COURAGEOUS RESPONSE

The world needs your yes! Move now!

You probably know this already, but let me remind you. Words, ideas, philosophies are not enough. They are powerless without action. In fact, you could open up to all three of the previous steps, but if you stop there, you will never fully claim your second chance.

Our "yes" to living fully alive means we move. We create. We build. We throw our whole hearts into creating the life we desire. Courageous response is needed, and that means taking steps, cultivating fresh activities, and building new relationships.

Activate your vision each day. Remember, you can't think yourself into new living; you have to live yourself into new thinking. The world needs your yes! Have courage and guts. You've got this! Make a move.

REFLECTIVE QUESTIONS:

What is the biggest fear you have about responding and taking action?

What low-risk, fairly easy change could you make today?

How can you engage your body with the ideas, dreams, and hopes swirling around in your head? What would that look like?

I SEE GOD AS A FRIEND WHO SMILES AND LAUGHS AND LIKES CUPCAKES.

HE IS THE LIFE AND GOD OF THE PARTY.

NOTES

Introduction: Three Seconds

1. Brennan Manning, *Abba's Child: The Cry of the Heart for Intimate Belonging* (Colorado Springs: NavPress, 2015), 42.
2. This story was communicated to me by my friend Jeff Brazil, who is part of a MacArthur Foundation–funded research effort at the University of California's Humanities Research Institute. A part of their research includes the study of alternative education frameworks with the focus on at-risk youth.
3. Richard Rohr, *Falling Upward: A Spirituality for the Two Halves of Life* (San Francisco: Jossey-Bass, 2011), 5–6.
4. Howard Zinn, "The Optimism of Uncertainty," in *The Impossible Will Take a Little While: Perseverance and Hope in Troubled Times,* ed. Paul Rogat Loeb (New York: Basic Books, 2014), 86.
5. Mary Oliver, "The Summer Day," in *New and Selected Poems* (Boston: Beacon Press, 1992), 94.
6. Quoted in Steve Reifenberg, afterword to *In the Company of the Poor: Conversations with Dr. Paul Farmer and Fr. Gustavo Gutierrez,* ed. Michael Griffin and Jennie Weiss Block (Maryknoll, NY: Orbis, 2013), 194–95.
7. John Kenneth Galbraith, *The Age of Uncertainty* (Boston: Houghton Mifflin, 1977), 96.

Chapter 1: Green Coats

1. Anne Lamott, *Bird by Bird: Some Instructions on Writing and Life* (New York: Anchor, 1994), 50, 28.
2. Atlas Obscura, "A Fake Village and a Colossal Flagpole: North Korea's Bizarre Propaganda Methods," *Slate,* October 14, 2013, www.slate.com/blogs/atlas_obscura/2013/10/14/a_fake_village_and_a_colossal_flagpole_north_korea_s_bizarre_propaganda.html.
3. LaDonna Witmer, "A Kingdom of Cardboard and Spoils," in Dieter Zander and LaDonna Witmer, *A Stroke of Grace* (Berkeley, CA: Dieter Zander, 2012), 25. Used by permission.

Chapter 2: Return Home

1. "Cynthia Occelli," Goodreads, www.goodreads.com/quotes/1013836-for-a-seed-to-achieve-its-greatest-expression-it-must.

2. Angela Morgan, "Utterance," in *Utterance and Other Poems* (New York: Baker & Taylor, 1917), 99.
3. Paul Young, "Where's God When Trailer," June 14, 2014, www.youtube.com/watch?v=u1PwvNNTzDo&feature=youtube.
4. Robert Farrar Capon, *The Parables of Grace* (Grand Rapids, MI: Eerdmans, 1988), 137.
5. Quoted in Jon Pareles, "Warren Zevon's Last Waltz," *New York Times,* January 26, 2003, www.nytimes.com/2003/01/26/magazine/warren-zevon-s-last-waltz.html.

Chapter 3: Dead Man's Party

1. Rainer Maria Rilke, *Letters to a Young Poet,* trans. Stephen Mitchell (New York: Random House, 1984), 34–35.
2. "Bureau of Justice Statistics, Reentry Trends in the U.S.: Recidivism," Office of Justice Programs, last modified June 13, 2016, www.bjs.gov/content/reentry/recidivism.cfm.
3. Scott Larson and Daniel L. Tocchini, *Groundwork: Preparing the Soil for God's Transformation* (Loveland, CO: Group, 2015).
4. Quoted in Scott J. Larson, "Teaching for Transformation in Today's Challenging Youth," Straight Ahead, www.straightahead.org/files/teaching_for_transformation_in_todays_challenging_youth.pdf.
5. Warren Hoge, "Finnish Prisons: No Gates or Armed Guards," *New York Times,* January 2, 2003, www.nytimes.com/2003/01/02/international/europe/02FINL.html?pagewanted=all.
6. "Five Prisons to Close as Falling Crime Rate Leaves Cells Empty," Dutch News.NL, March 21, 2016, www.dutchnews.nl/news/archives/2016/03/more-prisons-to-close-as-falling-crime-leaves-cells-empty.
7. Abbie Hoffman, *Revolution for the Hell of It* (1968; reprint, New York: Thunder's Mouth Press, 2005), 188.
8. Sam Dolnick, "Dance, Laugh, Drink. Save the Date: It's a Ghanaian Funeral," *New York Times,* April 11, 2011, www.nytimes.com/2011/04/12/nyregion/12funerals.html?_r=0.

Chapter 4: Be Brave with Your Story

1. Zora Neale Hurston, *Written by Herself,* vol. 1 of *Autobiographies of American Women: An Anthology,* ed. Jill Ker Conway (New York: Vintage, 1992), 51.
2. Guy Raz interview with Bernie Krause, "How Does Listening to Nature Teach Us About Changing Habitats?" KUOW, September 27, 2013, http://kuow.org/post/how-does-listening-nature-teach-us-about-changing-habitats.
3. Kurt Vonnegut to Mary Bancroft, April 5, 1972, in *Kurt Vonnegut: Letters,* ed. Dan Wakefield (New York: Delacorte, 2012), 181.

4. Fred Rogers, *The World According to Mister Rogers: Important Things to Remember* (New York: Hyperion, 2003), 167.
5. Dan B. Allender, *The Wounded Heart: Hope for Adult Victims of Childhood Sexual Abuse* (Colorado Springs: NavPress, 2008), 54.
6. Brené Brown, *Rising Strong* (New York: Spiegel & Grau, 2015), 43.
7. Ed Catmull with Amy Wallace, *Creativity, Inc.: Overcoming the Unseen Forces That Stand in the Way of True Inspiration* (New York: Random House, 2014), chapter 7.
8. Cheryl Strayed, *Tiny Beautiful Things: Advice on Love and Life from Dear Sugar* (New York: Vintage, 2012), 57.

Chapter 5: The Wonderful in the Weird

1. Richard Rohr, *Things Hidden: Scripture as Spirituality* (Cincinnati: St. Anthony Messenger Press, 2008), 25.
2. Jesus Culture, "Come Away," *Come Away* (Brentwood, TN: Capitol Christian Music Group, 2010).
3. "British Sterling Cologne," FraganceX, www.fragrancex.com/products/_cid_cologne-am-lid_b-am-pid_799m__products.html.
4. Cited in Carol Kinsey Goman, "Why You Should Reach Out and Touch Someone," *Forbes,* January 28, 2014, www.straightahead.org/files/teaching_for_transformation_in_todays_challenging_youth.pdf.

Chapter 6: Change the Mixtape

1. Bon Jovi, "Wanted Dead or Alive," *Slippery When Wet* (Mercury Records, 1986).
2. Pamela Weintraub, "The Voice of Reason," *Psychology Today,* May 4, 2015, www.psychologytoday.com/articles/201505/the-voice-reason.
3. Cited in Weintraub, "The Voice of Reason."
4. Cited in Weintraub, "The Voice of Reason."
5. Quoted in Weintraub, "The Voice of Reason."
6. Quoted in Weintraub, "The Voice of Reason."
7. Quoted in Weintraub, "The Voice of Reason."
8. *What About Bob?* directed by Frank Oz (Burbank, CA: Touchstone Pictures, 1991).
9. Tim Keller, *The Freedom of Self-Forgetfulness: The Path to True Christian Joy* (Leyland, Lancashire, UK: 10Publishing, 2012), 14.
10. Keller, *The Freedom of Self-Forgetfulness,* 26.
11. Keller, *The Freedom of Self-Forgetfulness,* 32.
12. Keller, *The Freedom of Self-Forgetfulness,* 37–38.
13. Koko Willis and Pali Jae Lee, *Tales from the Night Rainbow* (Honolulu: Night Rainbow Publishing, 1990).

Chapter 7: Accept Your Fifty-One Status

1. Shel Silverstein, "Fourth Place" in *Every Thing on It* (New York: HarperCollins, 2011), 55.
2. Amanda Scherker, "2nd-Grader's Cure for Playground Loneliness: A Buddy Bench," *Huffington Post,* December 3, 2013, www.huffingtonpost.com/2013/12/03/second-grader-buddy-bench_n_4378248.html.
3. Christian Bucks, "Buddy Bench," YouTube, December 6, 2013, www.youtube.com/watch?v=mlY0GE4DHro.

Chapter 8: De-Bacon Your Heart

1. Charles Passy, "Bacon Sales Sizzle to All-time High," *MarketWatch,* April 18, 2014, www.marketwatch.com/story/bacon-sales-sizzle-to-all-time-high-2014-02-11.
2. Arun Gupta, "Bacon as a Weapon of Mass Destruction," *Indypendent,* July 23, 2009, https://indypendent.org/2009/07/23/bacon-weapon-mass-destruction.
3. Quoted in Gupta, "Bacon as a Weapon of Mass Destruction."
4. Kate Bratskeir, "World Health Organization: Processed Meats Cause Cancer," *Huffington Post,* October 26, 2015, www.huffingtonpost.com/entry/world-health-organization-processed-meats-cause-cancer_us_562e1144e4b0aac0b8fd51b2; Colin Schultz, "The First Meal Eaten on the Moon Was Bacon," *Smithsonian,* April 8, 2014, www.smithsonianmag.com/smart-news/first-meal-eaten-moon-was-bacon-180950457/?no-ist; and "Bacon vs. Sex: 43% of Canadians Prefer the Pork," *Huffington Post,* April 19, 2010, www.huffingtonpost.com/2010/02/17/bacon-vs-sex-43-of-canadi_n_466513.html.
5. Sarah Hepola, "Bacon Mania," *Salon,* July 7, 2008, www.salon.com/2008/07/07/bacon_mania/.
6. David A. Kessler, *The End of Overeating: Taking Control of the Insatiable American Appetite* (New York: Rodale, 2009), 92–93.
7. Alan Watts, *The Book: On the Taboo Against Knowing Who You Are* (1966; reprint, New York: Vintage, 1989), 10.
8. See, among other works, Solomon Asch, "Forming Impressions of Personality," *Journal of Abnormal and Social Psychology* 41, no. 3 (July 1946): 258–90.
9. "Cardboard Stories|Homeless in Orlando," Rethink Homelessness, YouTube, June 26, 2014, www.youtube.com/watch?v=THxtcWNw3QA.
10. Bob Goff, Twitter, June 28, 2015, @bobgoff.
11. Quoted in Jim Forest, "The Spiritual Roots of Protest," in *Catholic Voices in a World on Fire,* ed. Stephen Hand (Raleigh, NC: Lulu, 2005), 180.
12. *Inside Out,* directed by Pete Docter and Ronnie del Carmen (Burbank, CA: Walt Disney Pictures, 2015).

Chapter 9: Leave the Garden of Shame

1. Lewis B. Smedes, *Shame and Grace: Healing the Shame We Don't Deserve* (New York: HarperCollins, 1993), ix.
2. Elizabeth Gilbert, *Committed: A Love Story* (London: Bloomsbury, 2011), 131.
3. "What's the Fattest Thing You've Ever Done?" Reddit, www.reddit.com/r/AskReddit/comments/284p3c/whats_the_fattest_thing_youve_ever_done/.
4. "What's the Fattest Thing You've Ever Done?" Reddit.
5. See Dog Shaming, dogshaming.com.
6. Madeleine Davies, "2013: The Year in Shaming," *Jezebel,* December 31, 2013, http://jezebel.com/2013-the-year-in-shaming-1492286697.
7. Jon Ronson, "When Online Shaming Spirals Out of Control," TED, June 2015, www.ted.com/talks/jon_ronson_what_happens_when_online_shaming_spirals_out_of_control.
8. Leonard Cohen, "Anthem," *The Future* (New York: Columbia, 1992).

Chapter 10: Be Beloved

1. James F. Masterson, *The Search for the Real Self: Unmasking the Personality Disorders of Our Age* (New York: Free Press, 1988), 67.
2. See Anti-Climacus (a pseudonym for Søren Kierkegaard), *The Sickness unto Death: A Christian Psychological Exposition for Edification and Awakening,* ed. Søren Kierkegaard, trans. Alastair Hannay (New York: Penguin, 1989), 144.
3. Laura K. Barnard and John F. Curry, "The Relationship of Clergy Burnout to Self-Compassion and Other Personality Dimensions," *Pastoral Psychology* 61, no. 2 (April 2012): 149–63.
4. Paul Vitello, "Taking a Break from the Lord's Work," *New York Times,* August 1, 2010, www.nytimes.com/2010/08/02/nyregion/02burnout.html.
5. James E. Côté and Charles G. Levine, *Identity Formation, Agency, and Culture: A Social Psychological Synthesis* (Mahwah, NJ: Lawrence Erlbaum, 2002), xi.
6. Timothy Keller with Kathy Keller, *The Meaning of Marriage: Facing the Complexities of Commitment with the Wisdom of God* (New York: Dutton, 2011), 48.
7. Carl G. Jung, *Modern Man in Search of a Soul,* trans. W. S. Dell and Cary F. Baynes (1933; reprint, New York: Harcourt Brace, 1955), 235.

Chapter 11: Banish Fear

1. Alix Spiegel and Lulu Miller, interview with Roger Hart, "World with No Fear," NPR, January 15, 2015, www.npr.org/2015/01/16/377517810/world-with-no-fear.

2. Spiegel and Miller, "World with No Fear."
3. Spiegel and Miller, "World with No Fear."
4. Spiegel and Miller, "World with No Fear."
5. Spiegel and Miller, "World with No Fear."
6. Spiegel and Miller, "World with No Fear."
7. Frank Furedi, *Culture of Fear Revisited: Risk-Taking and the Morality of Low Expectation* (New York: Continuum, 2006), 2–3.
8. Furedi, *Culture of Fear Revisited,* 37.
9. Barry Glassner, *The Culture of Fear: Why Americans Are Afraid of the Wrong Things,* 10th anniv. ed. (New York: Basic Books, 2009), xix.
10. Glassner, *The Culture of Fear,* xxv.

Chapter 12: Move from Bad Story to Backstory

1. Fariss Samarrai, "Rebels and Mean Girls Not So 'Cool' When Older, U.Va. Study Finds," UVAToday, June 12, 2014, https://news.virginia.edu/content/rebels-and-mean-girls-not-so-cool-when-older-uva-study-finds.
2. Kieran Corcoran, "Being Unpopular with the Opposite Sex at School 'Boosts Your GPA by 0.4,'" *Daily Mail* (UK), August 2, 2015, www.dailymail.co.uk/news/article-3182752/Being-unpopular-opposite-sex-school-boosts-GPA-0-4-Researcher-claims-ignored-education-end-smarter.html.
3. Chuck Pahlaniuk, *Haunted: A Novel of Stories* (New York: Doubleday, 2005), 205.
4. *The Incredibles,* directed by Brad Bird (Emeryville, CA: Pixar, 2004).
5. Joan Chittister, *Between the Dark and the Daylight: Embracing the Contradictions of Life* (New York: Image, 2015), 19.
6. Christine Caine, Twitter post, October 12, 2013, 7:38 a.m., @Christine Caine.
7. Quoted in Carl Koch, *Creating a Christian Lifestyle* (Winona, MN: St. Mary's Press, 1996), 217.
8. *Dirty Dancing,* directed by Emile Ardolino (Stamford, CT: Vestron Pictures, 1987).
9. Quoted in Grady Smith, "Robert Downey Jr. Asks Hollywood to Forgive Mel Gibson at American Cinematheque Awards," *Entertainment Weekly,* October 15, 2011, www.ew.com/article/2011/10/15/robert-downey-jr-forgive-mel-gibson.

Conclusion: New Endings

1. Brené Brown, "Owning Our History. Changing Our Story," n.d., brenebrown.com/owning-our-history-changing-our-story/.

Tips, Doodles, and Steps to Help You Rise Glorious

1. Lewis B. Smedes, *Shame and Grace: Healing the Shame We Don't Deserve* (San Francisco: HarperSanFrancisco, 1993).

ACKNOWLEDGMENTS

Jennifer, Jackson, and Taylor Foster. You are my beloveds.

Jud and Lori Wilhite for your friendship and unending encouragement.

Bill Townsend for your guidance, mentorship, and love. Thanks for rescuing me when I needed it so badly.

Scott Pace. You are the secret weapon, and I am grateful for your leadership and friendship.

The WaterBrook Multnomah team. I can't thank you enough for your belief in this message. Andrew Stoddard for being the best editor and encourager. Alex Field and Tina Constable for being such champions of this book. Beyond grateful.

Mom and Dad and Kristen. The Michalski Family and the Plouffe Family.

Kevin and Robin Small. Shannon Sedgwick-Davis. Brian and Jorie Johnson.

My friends and family at Central Christian Church. Your love lights up grace city.

The People of the Second Chance staff, team, and volunteers.

Justin Jackson for adding your brilliance to this book and helping me not give up. Jeff Brazil and Kaley Thompson. Eric Stanford. Jon Acuff.

Esther Fedorkevich and the Fedd Agency. You guys are rock stars!

Bob Goff for your belief in what I'm saying and for inviting me into your family.

Peter, Blake, and Bryce of PlainJoe Studios. Daley Hake. CJ Casciotta.

Thanks to Chloé du Plessis for the beautiful quote designs.

For all the churches and leaders who have let me share on your stage.

Jason Russell. Sam Larson. Josh Webb. Doug Slaybaugh. Jason Graves. Ryan O'Neal.

To my fellow hopesters, second chancers, and imperfectionists. You are why I love waking up each morning.

ABOUT THE AUTHOR

Mike Foster is the Chief Chance Officer at People of the Second Chance. He is a nationally recognized leader on helping people relaunch their lives and has been featured on *Good Morning America, The 700 Club,* and in the *New York Times.*

ACCESS THE

FREE "YOU RISE GLORIOUS" E-COURSE AT MIKEFOSTER.TV/RISE

Join Mike as he shares the strategies and tactics to rising glorious in your own life. Here's what you will learn:

The Four Steps to Maximizing Your Second Chance
How to Identify the Victim Mind-Set and Stop It in Its Tracks
Tips on How to Simplify Your Next Steps to Growth
How to Cultivate Self-Love on Hard Days

YOU RISE GLORIOUS

STUDY GUIDE &
GROUP MATERIALS

In this five-session group study, Mike shows us how to live in God's calling beyond our brokenness. This enables us to embrace our new identity as the beloved. Includes a study guide and video teaching.

Available Now at MikeFoster.tv

PEOPLE OF THE SECOND CHANCE

People of the Second Chance is a nonprofit organization guided by this lofty ideal: every person on earth deserves a second chance. We happily create helpful resources for not-so-perfect people.

OTHER RESOURCES BY MIKE FOSTER

FREEWAY

A NOT-SO-PERFECT GUIDE TO FREEDOM

Freeway is a small-group curriculum and sermon series to help people experience real freedom in their lives by going through a powerful 6-step process.

A NOT-SO-PERFECT GUIDE TO WHO YOU ARE AND WHY YOU'RE HERE

Wonderlife is a small-group curriculum and sermon series that takes people on an authentic journey through their not-so-perfect stories to find their sacred calling.

All resources for churches and imperfectionists exclusively at:

SECONDCHANCE.ORG

Rescue Lab is Mike Foster's 2-day workshop designed to teach you the skills and strategies to coach and counsel hurting people. With exclusive content and an interactive learning format, Rescue Lab will unleash your passion to impact people's lives forever.

RESCUE LAB WILL TEACH YOU TO:

Leverage your own story to help others
Develop awesome life-counseling skills
Establish self-care strategies and boundaries
Maximize your God-given gifts and abilities
Create confidence in your calling
Become a radical shamebreaker

To register for Rescue Lab visit:
SECONDCHANCE.ORG

CONTACT MIKE

MIKE.FOSTER@SECONDCHANCE.ORG

INSTAGRAM: @MIKEFOSTER2000

TWITTER: @MIKEFOSTER